GOD
AND
RACE

A Guide for Moving Beyond
Black Fists and White Knuckles

GOD
AND
RACE

JOHN SIEBELING

WAYNE FRANCIS

HarperOne
An Imprint of HarperCollinsPublishers

All Scripture quotations, unless otherwise indicated, are taken from the Holy Bible, New International Version®, NIV®. Copyright © 1973, 1978, 1984, 2011 by Biblica, Inc.™ Used by permission of Zondervan. All rights reserved worldwide. www.zondervan.com. The "NIV" and "New International Version" are trademarks registered in the United States Patent and Trademark Office by Biblica, Inc.™

GOD AND RACE. Copyright © 2022 by John Siebeling, Wayne Francis. All rights reserved. Printed in Canada. No part of this book may be used or reproduced in any manner whatsoever without written permission except in the case of brief quotations embodied in critical articles and reviews. For information, address HarperCollins Publishers, 195 Broadway, New York, NY 10007.

HarperCollins books may be purchased for educational, business, or sales promotional use. For information, please email the Special Markets Department at SPsales@harpercollins.com.

FIRST EDITION

Designed by Leah Carlson-Stanisic

Library of Congress Cataloging-in-Publication Data is available upon request.

ISBN 978-0-06-308722-4

22 23 24 25 26   FRI   10 9 8 7 6 5 4 3 2 1

Contents

PART ONE

Hope

Start at the End

BEGIN CREATING A HOUSE
THAT LOOKS LIKE HEAVEN

JOHN SIEBELING AND WAYNE FRANCIS

You have a problem.

It's a complicated problem with historical, political, and spiritual dimensions—and it's a big deal. We have the same problem, and so does everyone else in the world.

Racism is *real*, and it affects *everyone*.

The thing about complicated problems is there are no simple solutions. Approaching racial tension with simple solutions is like a heart surgeon stepping into surgery armed with a couple of Band-Aids and a "Get Well Soon" card.

One book is not going to fix centuries of pain, profiling, and privilege. However, although there are no simple solutions to this complex problem, we believe there is a simple starting point. If our country is going to start to heal from centuries of tension, it's going to be because we begin having civil conversations with people who don't look like us.

Conversations are the starting point because so much of the misunderstanding comes from a lack of perspective. The next time you are in the same room with someone, try this exercise. Hold this book up between you with the front cover facing you and ask them to describe what they see. Even though they are looking at the same book as you, they will describe the back cover. You are looking at the same object but from two different vantage points.

For the sake of the illustration, pretend you want to know what the back cover looks like but aren't able to turn the book around. What would you do? You wouldn't make something up in your head and assume you already know what it looks like. The way forward is to ask the right questions to the person who can see it and then listen to their perspective. You may not be able to see the back cover, but you can engage in a conversation with that person and let them paint a picture of it for you. Together, you can each gain a better understanding of the whole book.

That is a simple illustration with powerful implications. The truth is, no matter who you are, you have a limited vantage point. That's not a shot at you; it's an observation about humans. You are seeing every problem our world is facing from your perspective. Which is why so many racist remarks begin with

Why can't they just . . .

I don't understand why he doesn't . . .
If it were me, I'd already have . . .

But when we learn to have actual, mature conversations with people of other ethnicities, our perspectives and horizons are expanded. In this book, we want to give you a *guide* for not just starting conversations with people who don't look like you, but letting those conversations turn into friendships.

The starting point is simple, but that doesn't mean starting is simple. Learning how to have conversations about race is an art, and that art is what this book is all about. These conversations can be intimidating, but we'll be your *guides* and help you navigate the waters of race relations with confidence and grace.

Why are conversations about race (particularly in the *White-Black* tension) so scary to initiate and difficult to sustain? (By the way, we know racism is not solely a *Black* and *White* problem, but that is our context. Whatever ethnicity you are, whatever hardships you've experienced, we hope that by hearing about racism from our two perspectives, you'll be able to step into your arena and fight your fight with confidence and love.)

The *Black* and *White* tension is tense because we are inheriting centuries of pain and power struggles. Conversations work best when done with open hearts, open minds, and open hands. But hundreds of years into this struggle, it's not always easy to enter the conversation with open hands. The reason conversations can be so difficult and intimidating is because instead of coming to the discussion with open hands, we've brought *Black fists* and *White knuckles*.

Black Fists

WAYNE FRANCIS

I grew up with a lot more hair than I have today. Like many young Black men, I never left the house without my hair pick. If you don't know what a hair pick is, google it. We carried them around everywhere because you never knew when you might need it.

The handle at the end of my pick was a *Black fist*, a symbol that was made famous at the 1968 Summer Olympics, when Tommie Smith and John Carlos, two African American athletes, raised their fists during the medal ceremony. As the "Star-Spangled Banner" played, they put their fists in the air to stand in solidarity for the Black community. Ever since, the *Black fist* has become a symbol of standing up against the residue of segregation, slavery, and the systematic oppression that was (and still is) happening against Black people in our country.

I rocked my pick with pride. To me, the *Black fist* was a cool symbol of style and culture and was a beautiful sign of strength. The *Black fist* is retaliatory in its nature, and when you feel oppressed, fighting seems necessary.

Historically, the Black community has been oppressed. When being oppressed, the solution is not to give up or give in. Conforming or muting our Blackness is not the answer. The way forward is to be who we are. This isn't a book about ignoring centuries of oppression. This isn't a book about getting amnesia. Quite the opposite: if we want to get to where we want to be, we have to remember where we came from.

The question is, however, How do we move forward? I've heard it said that racism is prejudice plus power, whether you are trying to obtain it or maintain it. For the Black community, our journey has been an attempt to obtain power. From here, what's going to help more—open hands or clenched fists?

There is a time and a place for making a scene, but real power comes when we open our hands. We can have open-handed conversations without compromising our integrity. That's what I've learned from my friendship with John.

The first time I met John, I was on the heels of preaching a seven-minute sermon at the ARC Conference, an annual church planting conference. ARC (Association of Related Churches) has helped plant hundreds of churches all around the world, and its conference is always a highlight of my year. John walked up and introduced himself, but to be honest, I knew exactly who he was. He's on the leadership team of ARC, so he's kind of a big deal in the church planting world. Plus, I'd heard all about the success he had building a diverse church in Memphis.

At the time, I had been leading a church in New York for many years, aspiring to build a church like his, and though we were successful, it was a slow burn. I had mega-church dreams but was experiencing a bunch of mini-church nightmares!

John and his wife, Leslie, gave me a bunch of compliments about my sermonette and how they had a great time listening to me speak. I told them that I had heard about them for a while, and I wanted to check out their church. That's common small talk in the church world, but nothing conclusive hardly ever comes from it.

But John was different.

A few weeks later, I was on a plane to Memphis. We had a blast. The connection was easy and natural, and before I knew it, I was flying to Memphis every month. The Life Church quickly became my favorite church to be a guest speaker at—they made me feel right at home.

Behind the scenes, John and I were forming a true friendship. Honestly, it was the monthly BBQ fixes we bonded over, but I loved making him crack up with random jokes and impressions of Jamaican characters from my upbringing. And I loved how transparent I could be with him. Our conversations went so deep at times that I almost started packing scuba gear before my visits!

At the time, I didn't have a pastor, so my wife, Claudene (or Classy, as I started calling her while we were dating), and I asked the Siebelings to be our pastors. From there, our conversations just kept getting better until it felt like the pastoral relationship was morphing into a partnership. The day he opened his hands and invited us to be a part of the Life Church family was a big day. I was honored but hesitant. It's not easy to plant a church in the Northeast, but after a decade of hard work, we pulled it off.

We were a successful church, and the thought of letting it go was a bit daunting. To be honest, my fists were clenched around it a little too tight, but more on that later.

From day one, John made it clear that I don't have to fight for my place in our friendship. I am free to open my hands and be who God created me to be.

White Knuckles

JOHN SIEBELING

My parents gave me a gift. I grew up in the South, but they are from Wisconsin, and they raised me without a lot of the racial baggage I saw in my peers. I remember sleeping over at friends' houses and noticing a tangible difference between the way their parents talked about minority groups and the way mine did. My parents taught me how to love and respect everyone, regardless of the color of their skin, and because of that, I see diversity as an *opportunity* to open my hands instead of an *obstacle*.

Our nation is changing fast. Minority groups are quickly becoming the majority. Today, in the United States, more minority babies will be born than White babies, and according to Pew Research Center projections, by 2055 White people will no longer be the majority in our nation.[1] The truth is, you used to need the White vote to win an election, but things are changing, and if power is the goal, that is a threat. In his book *Why We're Polarized*, Ezra Klein says it this way: "White voters who feel they are losing a historical hold on power are reacting to something real. For the bulk of American history, you couldn't win the presidency without winning a majority—usually an overwhelming majority—of the white vote."[2] Things are shifting quickly, and many White Americans are still gripping to a long-standing paradigm of privilege that holds an advantage over people of color.

When someone is trying to hold on to the past, they are

reacting to something real. If it feels like something is slipping away, it's because it is. And people don't like change. It's human nature to remember the good old days and hold on to the past. But whenever you try to hold on to something too tightly, you don't leave any room for something new.

God is up to something in our nation. I worry that some people will miss out on it because they are trying to hold on to the past with *White knuckles*. I watch some people close their fists and try to hold on to the good old days because they are afraid the new things on the horizon will not be as good as the things in the past. But the Bible says, "perfect love drives out fear" (1 John 4:18). Our call is to love all people, and we can't do that with closed fists. We need to learn how to open our hands and surrender.

We can keep grasping for power, or we can let go. When we learn to open our hands, we'll find ourselves developing life-changing friendships with people who don't look like us. Wayne is one of those key friendships for me. The first time I saw him speak, I leaned over and told Leslie, "We need to meet that guy."

He packed more humor, energy, and alliteration into his seven-minute sermon than most pastors can do with thirty-five minutes. I always say I wasn't looking for him, and he wasn't looking for me, but we found each other that day, and it has been a divine journey ever since.

Whenever he came to Memphis, he brought so much joy and creativity that we always were sad to see him go. Honestly, I was hoping to recruit Wayne to join our team in Memphis. But the truth is, Wayne is a New Yorker through and through, and New York is where he needs to be.

But it also felt like we needed to collaborate. We were both passionate about racial healing, and Wayne was already pastoring a very diverse church. However, through a series of courageous conversations, we decided to bring his church in to join the Life Church family. We both let go of some things to come together. And here we are, a White guy and a Black guy partnering together to do something great in a racially fragmented nation.

It's been an amazing ride, and the result is something far greater than the sum of its parts. I remember Wayne telling me he was concerned about how our collaboration might be perceived. In fact, during his decision-making phase, some of his Black pastor friends even asked why he would "give" his church to a White man. There are many things I admire about Wayne, but one of them is his ability to stand in the tension between *Black* and *White*.

Wayne is a firm believer that God blesses unity.

And this book is proof that he is right.

We opened our hands and committed to collaboration, and the result has blown us away. Not only have we seen more life change, but we've also had a ton of fun along the way.

A House That Looks like Heaven

If we want to understand God's plan for race, we have to *start at the end*. In the book of Revelation, we get a glimpse into the end of the story: "After this I looked, and there before me was a great multitude that no one could count, from every nation, tribe, people and language, standing before the throne and before the Lamb" (Rev. 7:9).

Did you catch that?

Every tribe, tongue, and nation worshiping together. That's God's plan! The end of the story is a beautiful picture of a diverse group of people unified together before God. Let that fill you with *hope* today. No matter how divisive and polarized things may seem, we know the end of the story—we know where we will end up. One day, the church will be a diverse and unified group of humans all worshiping as one.

However, if you walk into a random church today, odds are that's not what you will see. There is a good chance it'll look more like one single tribe, tongue, and nation. Oftentimes, the words *God* and *race* don't seem to go together. They feel like two unrelated topics. But nothing could be further from the truth. Diversity and unity are pivotal pieces of God's plan. If we want the House of God to look like heaven, we need to accept that truth, celebrate it, and let it fill us with *hope* for the future.

Multiracial churches are not currently the norm, but we believe (with a lot of hard work) that we can get there together. And again, open-handed conversations are the starting point. The change may not happen overnight, but if we all devote ourselves to discussions and commit to learning how to learn from each other through healthy dialogue, we can work together to build houses that look like heaven.

That's the journey we are going on together.

This book is *a guide for moving beyond Black fists and White knuckles*. We want to help you open your hands and have fruitful and life-giving conversations about race. That journey begins in your own *heart*. In Part Two we'll talk about letting God search our hearts to get us ready to engage in these conversations. Then in Part Three we'll shift the focus externally and talk about your *household*—helping you invite diversity into your home and social circle. Finally, we'll end the book by talking in Part Four about inviting diversity into the *House of God*, and we'll lay out some strategies for creating a house that looks like heaven.

Along the way, we will get you ready to have open-handed conversations about race by discussing relevant issues from a *Black* and a *White* perspective. From here on out, we are going to alternate who writes each chapter. So if you've approached the race conversation from only one perspective, this book is for you. There are so many massive conversations surrounding race today; we want to give you a *guide* for understanding some of these issues from both a *Black* and a *White* perspective.

If you are brand-new to the race conversation and are scared to death you are going to say the wrong thing, this book is for you. We are going to equip you with the tools you need to enter into the fray with confidence.

If you are frustrated with the lack of attention your church is giving to race relations and are ready to make a positive change, this book is for you.

If you are a church leader unsure how to take the next step to help your congregation get it, this book is for you.

If you are unsure what to believe about the current state of racial tension in our country, this book is for you.

If a friend handed you this book and you are reading it only to do them a favor, then guess what? This book is for you too. Because no matter who you are or where you land spiritually or politically, we all have a part to play. There is *hope* for the future, but every one of us could use some more *guidance* for having open-handed conversations about *God and race*.

The truth is, as a nation, we are divided. We may not have

created this division, but we are living in it. If you still have a pulse, you have a responsibility to be the answer and the antidote to help push us forward toward the future God designed—a diverse future of unity and reconciliation. Let this book be a *guide* along the way because unless we make a solid, intentional choice to connect, understand, reach, and love one another, we will remain divided—and we can't afford to stay divided.

Let's loosen our grips, unclench our fists, open our hands, and come together.

Keep Walking

Above all, do not lose your desire to walk: every day I walk
myself into a state of well-being and walk away from every
illness; I have walked myself into my best thoughts, and I know
of no thought so burdensome that one cannot walk away from it.

—SØREN KIERKEGAARD

WAYNE FRANCIS

When I was eight years old, my life changed in a single afternoon.

I'm the son of Jamaican immigrants who came to the United States in the 1960s to pursue the American Dream and ended up in New York City. The Big Apple. There is a reason they call it "The City That Never Sleeps"; there is always something happening. And as a young kid, I never wanted to sleep either. Come to think of it, all these years later nothing has changed—I bring the party with me everywhere I go.

I was an innocent kid growing up in the Northeast Bronx. Redlining made it nearly impossible for most Black families to get preapproved for a loan in our neighborhood, so our block was predominantly White. For whatever reason, we were an exception. I never felt out of place walking around those streets, until one day, when my mother and I were walking down Pelham Parkway. We were heading to the bus stop to catch the 31 bus and go to the supermarket. As we walked, six White teenagers saw us coming from a long way off. It was a hot, lazy Monday afternoon in the Bronx, and apparently, they didn't have much going on. They were sitting on a brick wall along the sidewalk, pointing at us.

My mother is a strong Jamaican woman. She spotted them from a distance too and inched closer to me, grabbing my hand, but continued marching forward. Looking back, we had enough time to turn and find another route, but that was never an option in my mother's mind. We just kept walking. Pointing turned into snickering, which turned into laughter, and then into shouting.

They were calling us both the N-word, telling us to get out of their neighborhood. It was the first time I'd ever heard that word from a White person, and I was terrified. But my mom squeezed my hand a little harder and just kept walking.

She continued to stride right past them, and I did my best to follow suit.

Frustrated that they couldn't get a rise out of us, the ringleader decided to up the ante. He jumped off the brick wall, picked up a giant rock, and hurled it through the air. The rock found its target, striking my mother square in the back.

My mother grimaced in pain. Her body tightened up, and she froze for a moment. Behind us, the boys erupted in laughter. I was angry, confused, and sad all at once; my eight-year-old brain could not formulate a plan. Part of me wanted to run away. The other part of me wanted to run at the guys and turn up (I know no eight-year-old should ever pick a fight with six teenagers, but my emotions were taking over).

However, my mother had other plans, and whether she knew it or not, she was about to teach me one of the most important lessons of my life. A lesson I think about almost every day. A lesson that is so pivotal to this conversation, we've decided to make it our starting point on this journey toward racial unity. She looked over at me, and in her deep, calm Jamaican voice, she said, "Don't worry, jus' keep walkin', babee."

The Pain Problem

Blatant racism in broad daylight stings. It would be one thing if my mother and I had ventured into the wrong part of town at 2 a.m., but it was 2 p.m., and it was the street we traveled down every day. Those teenagers' intentions were clear as day.

One of the reasons our world erupted in 2020 after the deaths of Ahmaud Arbery in February and George Floyd in May was because they happened in broad daylight. We weren't left to wonder whether they were mistakes or accidents. They were intentional, and that hurts.

Have you ever had the rocks of racism hurled at you?

Have you ever seen someone throw the rocks of racism at someone else?

If you've ever experienced racism, you know how much it hurts. Unfortunately, the event that Monday afternoon on Pelham Parkway has happened millions of times, in millions of different ways, to millions of different people. From microaggressions to blatant acts of racism, our nation has experienced deeply rooted racism since day one.

It's no wonder open-handed conversations about race are so tricky. Every time I turn on the news or look at social media, it seems like there is another story of blatant racism. And each one hurts. Every time a friend tells me about a moment they were profiled, it hurts. Every time my daughters experience a microaggression, it hurts.

I wish I didn't get nervous every time I get a call from a Black friend, but I do.

I wish I didn't start sweating every time I get pulled over, but I do.

I wish I didn't have to teach my daughters the art of deescalation at such a young age, but I do.

After centuries of racism, our country has a major pain problem. My mother responded like a champion that day on Pelham Parkway. And looking back, that's one of the hardest parts about it for me. That wasn't the reaction of a rookie; it was the response of a seasoned veteran. That may have been my first run-in with racism, but it certainly wasn't my mother's first time around the block. My mother has seen and experienced her fair share of pain. Just like Jacob walked around with a limp after a night of wrestling with God, those words came at a price.

Before we can talk about having open-handed conversations about *God and race*, we have to be honest about what is keeping our fists closed. Suffer enough pain, and eventually, you'll lose your willingness to engage. Experience enough hurt, and eventually, you'll stop showing up. If you get beat and bruised every time you open your hands, you'll learn the art of clenched fists.

This chapter is about taking a cue from my mother. Persevering through the pain that racism causes is not easy, but you have to keep walking—you have to keep moving forward. If you don't, your pain problem will quickly become a paralysis problem.

The Paralysis Problem

I don't know if you remember, but 2016 was a bit of a polarizing year for our nation. In the midst of a polarizing election year, I decided to do a sermon series on politics. I've been a pastor for a long time, and my church and I have been through a lot together over the years, but I've never seen our church so stiff. People were staring at me like I was one word away from ending my career. I felt like I was tiptoeing through a field of land mines. I wasn't even getting political. I wasn't telling people who to vote for or which policies to pass; I was preaching "God wants the Oval Office in your heart!"

Crickets.

Nothing was landing, and everything was offensive. My inbox was filling, and our church was emptying. People were leaving left and right. The logical pastor would have backed off at that point, but one thing you have to know about me is I am a firm believer that we don't laugh enough. Sometimes we take all this stuff too seriously, so when things get tense, I start making jokes.

Our church is in Westchester County, a very liberal place north of the Bronx, and around that time, Donald Trump came out with the red "Make America Great Again" hat. I decided the right next move was to do a riff on the hat and create "Make Westchester Great Again" hats. My staff told me it was a terrible idea, and they were right. But I didn't listen. I made a hundred hats and took to the stage.

I thought I was about to crush it. Instead, I was crushed.

I jumped on the stage like Oprah. "You get a hat!" I yelled, tossing a hat to a lady in the front row. "And you get a hat! Everybody gets a hat!" You would've thought I'd released mosquitoes into the room. I'm not kidding. People were swatting them left and right. By the end of it, there were one hundred hats on the floor and not a single hat on a head.

Have you ever felt paralyzed?

That's how I felt trying to recover from that stunt. It was one of those days when I wondered whether I had missed my calling. People were shaking their heads at me, and all I could think about was how many of them I was seeing for the last time. The responses I got from people made me want to give up. It hurt, *and the product of pain is paralysis.*

The same principle applies to racism.

Our passion for unity can be stomped out quickly with the right amount of pain. Have you ever felt that way? Has the pain ever left you afraid of taking another step? If your answer is yes, I know the feeling. Over the years, the rocks of racism have come my way more times than I can count. Most of the time, they make me want to throw in the towel, stop fighting for diversity, settle down with a group of people who look like me, and call it a day. But if unity is the goal, paralysis is a problem. We don't have time to let awkward interactions or past mistakes paralyze us—*we must keep walking.*

But before we talk about how to do that, let's be honest: there's still another layer to this problem.

The Perfection Problem

Unless you've been living under a rock, you've heard the phrase *cancel culture.* If I disagree with your point of view, particularly regarding gender, race, or politics, I can decide to block you out. You no longer matter. You are no longer a part of my people group. Your opinion is disqualified, and this conversation is over. In other words, you are canceled.

And this isn't just some schoolyard bickering. Thanks to Twitter and other social media platforms, cancel culture is ruining people's lives. Ask anyone who has been canceled; it is incredibly challenging to come back from. You can build something for years, and then in one moment, it can be aggressively taken away from you. Obviously, people need to be held accountable for their words, but these days, you can be canceled for anything. I mean, food is now getting canceled for God's sake. Food. How do you cancel food?

Trust me, I get the temptation. In Chapter 1, I mentioned that the Black fist is a symbol of power. Cancel culture feels good because it empowers people. As *Vox* magazine columnist Aja Romano once said, "Cancel culture can serve as a corrective for the sense of powerlessness that many people feel."[1]

Here's a question: Have you canceled anybody recently? If

so, what was your motivation? Was it panic? Was it because you felt like that was the only power you had to make a difference? It seems like we put so much vitriol into calling each other out when we disagree with a person's stance instead of walking with or listening to them. How many more news anchors, magazines, companies, social media influencers, or inanimate objects do we have to cancel before we start talking to one another?

If that last paragraph triggered you, you might be ready to cancel us. But before you throw this book at your dog and take to Twitter, my challenge is to listen to what I am saying. I am a Black pastor who leads a racially diverse church and desperately wants to see reconciliation in this country, but every time I get on stage, I'm worried about being canceled from both sides. If I don't address certain issues at just the right moment, I'm concerned the Black community will jump online and talk about how I'm not woke enough. And yet if I don't phrase things just the right way, I'm worried the White community will tweet about how I'm a part of the problem. Or even worse, they'll leave our church and make our battle for diversity even harder. Again, accountability is important, but how will we ever have open-handed conversations about race if we are worried about being canceled every other word?

Cancel culture has created a perfection problem. *As long as perfection is a prerequisite for progress, we will stay paralyzed.*

The standard is perfection, which means unless you can talk about racism perfectly, you should keep your mouth shut entirely. That type of atmosphere is not conducive to healthy, open-handed relationships. What relationship has ever flourished with that mentality? Imagine if I told my wife, "You know I'm a little afraid I'm going to hurt you, so instead, I'm going to stay silent for several decades." That wouldn't go over well.

Here's one of the most common phone calls I get from my White friends:

"Hey Wayne, I-I-I have a question for you."

"Sure man, what's going on?"

"Well, I'm kinda embarrassed to ask."

"Just ask."

"Okay," they say, taking a deep breath. "Should I say 'Black' or 'African American'?"

I'm telling you, I get that question every week. My White friends get hung up there all the time. And I get it. These days, in the age of cancel culture, one wrong word will ruin you. If I were White, I'd be asking the same question. But semantics are a tool to get people to avoid the conversation. Saying the exact right thing is not nearly as crucial as entering into a relationship and jumping into the conversation.

God created us for community, so before you get caught up in semantics, learn to look for similarities. We are made for the amazing, long-lasting, grueling, painful, but beautiful process of learning how to exist with each other. Cancel culture is a quick fix. Let's be real: It's way easier to dismiss people than it is to deal with people. It's easier to just jump ahead to the next person than to try to stay in the trenches with people. It's easier to divide than it is to deal—and it's been that way for thousands of years.

The Original Cancel Culture

When Jesus walked the earth, he constantly had to deal with a slightly different type of cancel culture. There was a group of religious leaders named the Pharisees who had a knack for creating division. Their name literally translates as "set apart," and they walked around like they were better than everyone else.

One day, the Pharisees caught a woman in the act of adultery. As if the humiliation of being caught in the act wasn't enough, they dragged her into the temple courts to stone her to death. *Because for thousands of years, humans have been throwing rocks at people they don't understand.*

This was the original cancel culture crew. There are many reasons you may end up in someone else's tent, but instead of getting to know the woman and finding out more about the events leading up to her mistake, they decided it was time to cancel her.

Permanently.

The Pharisees had their fists tightly clenched around the rocks they planned to throw at the woman. They demanded perfection from her, but since she fell short, she sat paralyzed in the temple courts—awaiting her death. But then Jesus entered the picture and stood between the woman and the stone-throwers, uttering his famous words, "Let any one of you who is without sin be the first to throw a stone at her" (John 8:7). The cancel culture crew was stumped. They felt great about themselves while they were focusing on someone else's mistakes, but as soon as Jesus flipped the script and made them take inventory of their own lives, they didn't know what to do. They were fine demanding perfection from someone else, just as long as no one demanded perfection from them. One by one, they logged off Twitter—I mean, they opened their hands, dropped their rocks, and walked away.

That's the power of unclenched fists: you can't throw rocks with open hands.

Critiquing others has always been a convenient way to avoid our pain, but the beautiful and brilliant thing about Jesus is he loves us too much to fall into that trap. It turns out, Jesus did come to cancel something: "You were dead because of your sins and because your sinful nature was not yet cut away. Then God made you alive with Christ, for he forgave all our sins. He canceled the record of the charges against us and took it away by nailing it to the cross" (Col. 2:13–14, NLT).

Jesus is the answer to the perfection problem! He didn't come to cancel people; he came to cancel debts. While the mob was looking at the sin, hell-bent on canceling the woman, Jesus was looking at the woman, hell-bent on canceling the sin. Jesus may not have liked the woman's actions, but he didn't write her off as a person. But then on the other side of the equation, Jesus may not have liked the Pharisees, but he never wrote them off either. He almost always disagreed with them, but he also engaged with them. He never canceled the Pharisees; he thought about their questions and returned the favor with questions of his own.

And if you are a follower of Jesus, what if you learned to do the same?

What if instead of canceling the person who lashed out at you, you took some time to get to know them?

What if instead of turning your back on someone who hurt you, you gave them a second chance?

What if instead of writing people off when you disagreed with them, you asked them questions and tried to understand their perspective?

Jesus had a knack for walking into complex problems and finding the solutions no one else could think of. He didn't come to offer simple solutions—in fact, his solution cost him his life—but as he went, he did live by a few simple rules that helped him persevere through the persecution so he could *keep walking!*

Likewise, instead of looking for simple answers to complex problems, how about a simple rule? *Respect.* Every person, regardless of race, gender, or socioeconomic status, would like respect. Don't get bogged down by all the other rules you might think of; just start with respect. You'll be amazed at how much common ground you find with people when you start that way.

Before you get caught up in semantics, look for similarities.

Keep Walking

Cancel culture has created a perfection problem, but since no one is perfect, we all feel paralyzed, plus pain just throws gasoline on the fire. And then John and I have the gumption to come along and tell everyone to open their hearts and their hands and just get along. It almost seems laughable, right? Which is why we aren't doing that.

When I was coming up through school, math was never my strong suit. I've always been more of a word guy. But what every subpar math student knows about the textbooks is that the answers to all the odd questions are in the back of the book (or at least they used to be). I knew enough math to know that, guaranteed, I'd get half the questions right, which sounded just about sufficient to me.

This book doesn't work like that. This isn't a textbook—it's a *guide.* The answers aren't in the back. And if you just flipped to the end to check, welcome back. Let me assure you, there are no easy ways for a bunch of imperfect people to fix centuries of pain and paralysis; instead, this book is an invitation to join the journey.

The most powerful part of the Pelham Parkway story was not the Monday afternoon; it was the Tuesday that followed. The N-words, the rock, and the faces of those boys are etched into my memory forever, but so is the fact that we went back the next day and then again the day after that. Pelham Parkway is where we caught the 31 bus, and my mother wasn't about to let the pain or the fear change who we were. She felt the pain, but instead of letting it paralyze her, she kept walking. She didn't cancel Pelham Parkway, and she didn't cancel those teenagers. My mother wasn't just giving lip service to her words; she lived them out. She kept walking, and what we are willing to walk away from paves the best path toward what we should be walking toward.

If you are looking for a quick fix, let me save you some time—you've come to the wrong place. That's not what this book offers. Instead, it offers something better: hope for the future; space to acknowledge your pain, paralysis, and imperfections; and help so that you can keep walking.

We have to keep walking the walk.

And talking the talk.

Even when it hurts. Especially when it hurts. Because walking can heal us from the words that have hurt us. Hippocrates said it best: "Walking is man's best medicine."

I'm not suggesting we need to become walking target practice—that's weakness. But I believe that the same security I felt walking with my mother is possible for you when you learn to walk with your heavenly Father.

Walking humbly with God isn't a sign of weakness; it's the secret of strength. And you'll need all the strength you can get because open-handed conversations about race are not for the faint of heart. They are not for people who run *away* from pain or pretend everything is perfect. They are reserved for those who are willing to run *through* the pain and embrace the mess. I believe you are one of those people, which is why you are reading this book. *So let's keep walking forward together.*

To this day, I can still hear my mother's nurturing words. Over the years, the rocks of racism have been hurled at me more times than I can count. And trust me, I'm not immune to it. It hurts. I hate it. And a part of me always wants to retaliate. But my mother gave me a gift, a memory with some mileage that I've kept stored away deep in my heart. Each time the rocks of racism come my way, making me want to either shut down or turn around and start fighting, I hear my mother's words ringing in my soul, and I know exactly what I need to do: *Jus' keep walkin', babee.*

Get Ready

BECOME THE TYPE OF PERSON WHO STANDS UP AGAINST RACISM

Bad men need nothing more to compass their ends than
that good men should look on and do nothing.

—JOHN STUART MILL

JOHN SIEBELING

Summers in Louisiana are not for the faint of heart. The heat is bad, but the humidity is worse. One day, when I was about ten years old, my father and I stopped by Bonaparte's Fried Chicken after church. Apparently, everyone else had the same idea because the line was out the door.

The only person working the counter was an older African American lady. She was working as diligently as she could, but she couldn't keep up with the rush. Despite her best efforts, the line kept growing longer and longer. And the air-conditioning must have been broken because the hot summer sun was turning Bonaparte's into a sauna.

Hunger and heat have an odd way of bringing out the worst in people, and before long, the crowded room began to murmur. I could feel the tension rising. By the way, us church folks don't have the best reputation in the restaurant world. I know some waiters who call Sunday afternoon the "punishment shift" because they know they are bound to get impatient, rude people who won't tip well. That's a subject for another book, but can we please tip well? And remember: a smile never hurt.

While my father and I stood uncomfortably in the line, waiting our turn and wondering if the AC was ever going to turn back on, the guy right behind us reached his breaking point. The remarks started under his breath but quickly picked up steam. Eventually, he directed his attention to the African American lady behind the counter.

"Hey, *girl*!" he sneered. "Think you could move a little faster?"

My dad straightened up, his jaw tightened, his muscles tensed, and he spun around to look the guy in the eye.

"Now, *that's enough*!" he said, lifting his hand and taking a stand. "There's no reason for you to talk to her like that."

The two men stared at each other. From my young perspective, they might as well have been heavyweight fighters waiting for the sound of the bell. The rest of the restaurant was silent; all I could hear was the sound of my own heart beating out of my chest. I thought there was about to be a fight right in the middle of the room.

Finally, the other man looked away, grumbling. When we got to the front of the line, I could see the pain behind the woman's eyes. It was clear this was not the first time she had experienced those types of words. She mouthed the words *thank you* to my father, and he nodded.

My father was a professor who spent most of his time in the

laboratory. But when we got into the car, he sounded more like a social rights activist as he began to explain to me everything that had just happened. It was my first time really hearing about the history of our nation, and the racial baggage still around today. We talked about how the South had made progress, but there was still baggage and tension. He explained how historically, a White person calling a grown African American a *boy* or *girl* was derogatory and racist. That man wasn't just complaining. He was using a racial slur.

My head was spinning. I grew up in a predominantly White neighborhood, and only a few Black kids went to my school, but the thought of treating anyone as lesser of a human was baffling. Suddenly, the world wasn't quite as friendly as I had thought. That experience marked my life. As we drove home, with the sweet smell of fried chicken wafting through our car, I realized something we all have to come to terms with eventually. Racism is real, and there will come moments in my life when I have to take a stand and say, "That's enough!" It's not a matter of *if*; it's a matter of *when*. That day, I realized my job is to make sure I am ready for those moments when they come.

Nairobi

The fight for racial unity became personal for my wife, Leslie, and me when we moved to Nairobi, Kenya. We were newlyweds at the time and felt called to be missionaries in Africa, serving our pastors, Don and Amy, who were leading Nairobi Lighthouse Church. We packed an overseas container and headed off with a one-way ticket to Africa.

Our time there was special. We loved every minute. Nairobi was home. I could tell you story after story about all the amazing things God did, but what has stuck with us all these years later is the relationships and friendships we formed.

In school, I had learned about the Atlantic slave trade. When I read about it in books, I thought it was a terrible thing, but when Africans became my friends and my family, and I experienced their warm hospitality and rich ancestry, the thought of them being ripped out of their homes and torn from their families made me sick. For Leslie and me, Kenya turned sympathy into empathy. It's amazing what proximity does.

Nairobi left a mark on us. Pastors Don and Amy are a White couple, a minority in Kenya, yet through hard work and open hands, Nairobi has not only accepted them, but also embraced them. The people love them. We knew whenever the time came for Leslie and me to return to the States and plant a church, we wanted to create the same sort of space: where everyone is well received, and diversity is a pillar. Eventually, the day came. We had a feeling we were supposed to be in Memphis, Tennessee, and we couldn't shake it. And so, twenty-five years ago, we packed our bags, said several tearful goodbyes, and headed to Memphis to plant The Life Church.

A "Diverse" Church

When we first started telling family, friends, neighbors, and acquaintances about our next endeavor to go plant a church in Memphis, one White woman Leslie knew said, "You know, there are lots of Black people there." We found that so ironic because that woman knew we had been living in Kenya all those years. That's a picture of trying to hold on to the past with *White knuckles*—as if, in her mind, Black people living on a different *continent* seemed thinkable, but Black people living in her *community* seemed unthinkable. It became clear to us that helping people move beyond *White knuckles* would be a slow, long, but important endeavor.

Arriving in Memphis was overwhelming. We knew we were supposed to plant a diverse church, but we had no idea how. In those early days, our church brochure said we were a diverse church, but the truth is, we started very White. By the way, church leaders, the question is not "How diverse is your church?"; the question is "Does your church reflect the demographics of your city?"

When we started, our church was 100 percent White in a city that was more than 60 percent Black. We wanted to be a diverse church; the only thing missing was all the diversity. But instead of being *discouraged* by our reality, we were *encouraged* by the potential of what our church could be. We decided it was time to *get ready*. In order to have a diverse church, we needed to know what type of church people of other skin colors would love to be a part of, so we got to work. We became students of our city, and anytime we met people who didn't look like us, we sat with them, asked them questions, and learned as much as we could about how we could help our church be a place they were proud to call home.

We'll unpack this more as we go, but today, through a lot of hard work, we can proudly say we have a church that looks like our city. It hasn't been easy, and we've made our fair share of mistakes (which we will tell you all about). But today, the demographics of our campuses are very similar to the demographics of the city they are in. And not just in Memphis; the same is true for all our other lead pastors around the world. Our leadership team is a diverse group, and it's so inspiring watching them build in a cultural context where they can thrive.

But again, we weren't always that way. Leslie and I knew what we wanted—a church that matched our city's demographics— but there was a massive gap between what we wanted and what we had. If you've ever felt overwhelmed by the mountain standing in front of you, I know how you feel. If you've ever doubted whether or not you'd ever be able to get there and had no idea where to start, you are in good company.

When we drove into Memphis, we knew diversity would be an essential piece of our church. But it wasn't until we got settled in and began to learn a little more about the history of the city that we began to see just how crucial it would be. It wasn't just the humidity making us sweat; it was the hotbed of racial tension.

The Sanitation Strike

Most of the moments that stand out from history are moments when someone is brave enough to stand up and say *that's enough*. Those are the breaking points that bring about change.

For Memphis, one of the big breaking points came in 1968, at the tail end of the civil rights movement. Although the city was making progress, things were still very far from fair, especially in the workplace. It was nearly impossible for an African American to find a stable career. Most of them ended up working the dangerous and difficult jobs, for far less money than their White counterparts.

One example was the Memphis sanitation department. The pay was so low that several Black employees were still qualifying for welfare and relying on food stamps even though they were working full time.[1] But every complaint fell on deaf ears, so they kept their heads down and worked hard.

On one horrible rainy day in February, Echol Cole and Robert Walker were in the back of a garbage truck when the compressing piston malfunctioned, crushing both men. The city refused to pay either family any death benefits, even though Walker left behind a pregnant wife and five children.[2]

That day was the breaking point; on February 12, 1968, the Memphis sanitation strike began. After years of neglect and abuse, thirteen hundred Black men said *that's enough* and walked out.

Their demands were simple: fair pay and safer working conditions. But unfortunately, the mayor of Memphis did not want to hear it. Instead of listening, he dug his heels in and doubled down, trying to hold on to the status quo with White knuckles.

When Martin Luther King Jr. caught wind of the strike, he traveled to Memphis to join the cause. On April 3, 1968, he stood up at the Mason Temple and gave a famous speech called "I've Been to the Mountaintop" to the sanitation workers.

We have a member in our church, Mr. Curtis, who was there that historic night. Whenever I ask him about it, he gets a little twinkle in his eye. His face lights up, and he talks about how electric it was inside the auditorium. He remembers the excitement in the air the moment Dr. King started talking, seeing the promised land, and the weight everyone felt when he told them he might not get there with them.

That's the last speech Dr. King ever gave. He was assassinated the next day right outside the Lorraine Motel in downtown Memphis.

In the speech, he gave listeners a call to keep going, saying, "We've got to give ourselves to this struggle until the end. Nothing would be more tragic than to stop at this point in Memphis. We've got to see it through."[3]

Dr. King saw something starting in Memphis. He had *hope* for the future, so he took a stand for the city. And like most great prophets, it cost him his life. Even though he may be gone, his spirit lives on. To this day, his dream continues to pull our nation forward toward justice and equality. Dr. King had a dream that sparked a revolution. And it all started when he *took a stand* and declared, *that's enough.*

His swan song is a perfect reminder that we need to keep the fire burning. A movement started in Memphis all those years ago, and we need to see it through. Dr. King's words have haunted me in the best way for my twenty-five years in this city. I want to make sure we keep going. Leslie and I are honored and humbled to be a part of the ongoing movement toward racial healing in our city. We get to play a small role in helping Memphis look a bit more like heaven, and I can't think of anything I would rather do.

Turning Tables

————————

That's enough moments are expensive. They cost us something. They may cost us our reputations, friendships, jobs, and sometimes even our lives.

For Jesus, it cost him all of those things.

When he rode into Jerusalem on a donkey during the final week of his life, his first stop was the temple. The temple was a sacred space for Jewish men and women. It was the place God's presence dwelled. It was the place they went to worship, pray, and offer sacrifices. But most important, it was a place reserved only for Jews. They hung signs on the entrance to the temple forbidding outsiders from going any farther and named the very outer part the Court of the Gentiles (non-Jews).

Most scholars believe all the temple vendors set up their tables in the Court of the Gentiles. Imagine you were a gentile in the first century who was wrestling with life's biggest questions. If you traveled to the temple in search of some answers, the first thing you would see is a sign forbidding you from going past the outer courts, and then you would notice that the little bit of space you did have was turned into a gift shop. That is not a very welcoming space, and it certainly isn't conducive to a spiritual experience.

The Jewish people of Jesus's day were resisting people from the outside, intentionally blocking them from making their way in, making it nearly impossible for outsiders to experience God. The temple was supposed to be a place of prayer, but when Jesus walked in, he saw a bunch of vendors and money changers blocking the area where gentiles could worship.

This was a racial issue.

When Jesus saw what they were doing, he had a *that's enough* moment. Besides his agony on the cross and his anguish in the Garden of Gethsemane, what followed is the most intense we see Jesus being in scripture. He created a whip out of cords and strolled into the temple to create a scene. Filled with righteous anger, he cracked the whip and overthrew tables, sending doves flying and coins scattering. It was utter chaos.

Interestingly enough, our modern churches have had a similar problem. We'll talk more about this as we go, but one of the reasons the Black church even exists is because not too long ago, Black people were not allowed to worship alongside White people.

While most churches today aren't strategically prohibiting people of color from coming to their buildings, it is still happening in subtle ways. From our brochures, to our websites, to even our style of worship, we are guilty, at times, of failing to create literal and virtual welcome mats for diversity.

Jesus overturned the tables because of where they were set up. In recent years, my friends of color have told me that although it has become common to see people of color singing onstage or volunteering in church lobbies, it's rarer to see them involved in upper-tier leadership outside of the Black church. Unfortunately, this matches what we often see in secular culture, with people of color occupying a small margin of upper-tier management although so many African Americans are qualified for the same role.

People of color want and deserve a seat at the table. So if the tables aren't set up to welcome all people, it may be time to overturn them. Sometimes in the face of injustice, we have to *get ready* to take a stand and say *that's enough*. We have to be willing to confront the disrespect of what's sacred. We have to stand up for human beings when they are treated like they don't matter. Learning to do that has been a process for me, but I'm thankful for people who have come before me to pave the way.

My father's actions that afternoon in Bonaparte's Fried Chicken was about something bigger than two men staring each other down; it was about an entire history of racial tension in the South. Dr. King's trip to Memphis was more significant than the sanitation strike. It was a sign of solidarity to show an entire country that no one was fighting this battle alone. And what Jesus did in the temple was not just a religious statement; it was a declaration that all people are precious in God's sight, which means we should make room for everyone in the House of God.

If you are tired of acting like racism isn't a problem, sick of staying silent, and done with deferring the solution to someone else, Wayne and I want to share with you some practical thoughts about *getting ready* to take a stand and say *that's enough*.

No More Acting like This Is Not a Problem

The journey to open-handed conversations about race begins in your *heart*. Before we run off and talk about all the ways we can change the world, we first need to look inward. In Part Two, we take a deep internal dive and talk about hot button issues like privilege and profiling, allowing you to search your own *heart* in the process.

My father was a serious man, always immersed in his studies, but because his *heart* was in the right place, he also had time for everyone. When he passed away, I took a moment at his funeral to look around the room at all the different people he had influenced during his years. The head of the Centers for Disease Control and Prevention was sitting a few rows behind me. She flew in from Atlanta to honor my dad, who had done so much in his field. Willy, the Black janitor from my father's building, was sitting another row over. Behind Willy sat two families of Cajun turtle farmers from deep Louisiana (that's a story for another day). My point is, my dad made room for everyone. My father was far from perfect, but he never looked down on anyone for the color of their skin. Part Two is about doing the tough internal work so people will say the same thing about us.

No More Silence

Too many of us are content to say *good enough* instead of *that's enough*.

We feel like it's *good enough* that we aren't racist or don't hang out with racist people. But *good enough* is not enough. This isn't a book about how to not be a racist; it's a book about using your voice to *take a stand* and be antiracist!

Part Three is about your *household*. More specifically, it is about learning to use your voice to influence those you care about the most. Whether it's to your family, your friends, or the people you interact with on social media, you have something to say; in this part, we get practical and teach you how to say it well. When your moment comes to stand up for what's right, what are you going to do? Will you be ready to *take a stand*?

If the current racial climate you find yourself in is heating up, you may be sweating more than an after-church rush on a muggy Louisiana summer day. But don't worry; we are going to get practical and teach you to keep your cool as you speak up.

No More Deferring the Solution to Someone Else

Finally, in Part Four, we shift our focus to the *House of God*. Unfortunately, parts of the church have remained silent about racism for far too long. It's time to *get ready* to say *that's enough*. The church is God's plan for reconciliation in this world. In Part Four, we discuss our role, including what it looks like for both church leadership and the congregation to jump in and help.

The disciples didn't know what to do with Jesus the day he walked into the temple and made a scene. They looked at each other, wondering if this was the same guy who fed the masses, cast out demons, and welcomed everyone. And then one of them remembered the psalmist's words: "Zeal for your house consumes me" (Ps. 69:9).

Do people say the same about us?

You know the feeling you get when your own house isn't in order, and a visitor comes over? When you feel like you have to make balancing statements about your kids or how you've been really busy? Do we have the same urgency to speak up for the church? Are we passionate about letting visitors know there are some issues some people have stayed silent on for too long? You feel that about your home because you take personal responsibility for it. Are you ready to do the same for the House of God? In Part Four, Wayne and I help the church take steps to create a house that looks like heaven.

Are You Ready?

In the very beginning, Leslie and I were frustrated by how uniform our "diverse" church was. It's normal to feel like the mountain in front of you is too high to ever climb, but the only thing to do is start where you are and take the first step forward. In the beginning, all we had was a vision. However, we kept taking steps, and little by little, things started to change. And today, we proudly get to be a part of a very diverse church!

Are you ready to *take a stand*?

Are you ready to say *that's enough*?

My father was able to *take a stand* that day in Bonaparte's because, in his *heart*, he cared more about the woman behind the counter than his reputation. Are you ready to say *that's enough* to the bigotry or bitterness in your *heart*?

The men who bravely stood for their family and friends in the sanitation strike said *that's enough*, and households in Memphis and all around the world benefited from their bravery. Are you ready to do the same?

Jesus had a zeal for his father's house, and as the church, we should carry the same passion. Are you ready to say *that's enough* and help the church lead the way toward racial healing?

If your answer is no to any of those questions, stick with us; we will get there together. Enough is enough. It's time to join Jesus in the reconciliation of all things.

Let's start with the *heart*.

WHAT'S HOLDING YOU BACK?

This book is a guide for moving beyond Black fists and White knuckles, so at the end of each part, we're including a practical exercise called "Open Your Hands."

The best place to start is by addressing the fears, worries, or concerns you may have for working through the rest of this book. In Parts Two, Three, and Four, we challenge you to take an honest look at your life and the role you are playing to build a diverse house that looks like heaven. Before we get there, take a moment and be honest about any fears that may be holding you back as you contemplate studying and discussing the issue of race with others.

Having open-handed conversations about race can be scary. Some people may be nervous about what they will discover in their own lives. Others may be anxious about getting out of their comfort zone, experiencing new cultures, and meeting new people. Whatever it is for you, remember, if having open-handed conversations about race were easy, everyone would be doing it, and we wouldn't need to write this book.

Fear is real, but it thrives in the dark. Taking a moment to talk about it is like turning the light on in a dark room. It may not make the fear go away, but it helps you see it for what it is, and chances are, you will realize it isn't nearly as scary as you thought it would be. Take a few minutes to process through your fears by answering these questions. If you are going through this book with a friend or a group, take some time to talk through everyone's answers to these questions together.

What is your first reaction when you hear the discussion will be about race?

Is this subject easy for you to talk about, or does it make you nervous? Why do you think that is?

Is there any specific topic you are anxious about addressing? If so, which one?

What are your concerns about how others will react if you share freely your views on race?

Have you ever talked about race with people from a different race or ethnicity? If so, what was that like?

What is the biggest fear or concern holding you back from fully embracing this exploration of and discussion about race?

PART TWO

Heart

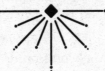

The journey toward racial healing starts in your *heart*. It's easy to sit in the grandstands and throw stones; it's much harder to look inward and get honest about the condition of your *heart*. Internal work is not easy, but it's necessary because we are never going to heal what we aren't willing to confront.

These days we have lots of people to blame for the injustice in the world. Social media allows us to highlight blatant acts of racism and talk to our friends about how wrong they are. It enables us to expend all our energy attacking the public figures, the politicians, the police, and the pastors. There is a time and place for all of those things, but open-handed conversations start with *you*.

King David understood this principle. He was the king of Israel and had his fair share of fires to put out and people to confront, but listen to the words of his prayer:

Search me, God, and know my heart;
    test me and know my anxious thoughts.
See if there is any offensive way in me,
    and lead me in the way everlasting. (Ps. 139:23–24)

Before he addressed the external, he first asked God to search his *heart*. We call David a man after God's *heart* because he took the time to let God search it.

But be warned, David's prayer should be reserved only for the brave souls who are ready to go there with God. Are you willing to let God search through all the dark rooms in your *heart*? The "storage rooms" where you've dumped all the old pain you never want to see again? The locked rooms where you've stashed your unforgiveness? Or even those hidden spots where you hold on to bitterness because you like having an excuse not to move forward?

In this part, we take an honest look at the racial climate of the United States. We are going to ask the difficult questions about profiling and privilege. But remember: the point is to give you space to take inventory of what is going on in *your heart*. Internal work isn't sexy. It doesn't make for a great post, and it won't get your name in the history books. But it is a necessary first step. Many people try to jump straight to solutions before they work on their own *hearts*, and the result is ineffectiveness and burnout. The journey starts in your *heart*.

If you want to be a man or a woman after God's heart, you have to let God search it and take out anything that is not supposed to be there. Ask any heart surgeon: heart work is neither comfortable nor clean, but it saves lives. If you are ready to let God get to work, pray this prayer with us:

Lord, search my heart and see if there is any offensive way in me. Reveal the places where I need to repent, and give me the strength to forgive when I need to forgive.

Feel the Burn

**IMMERSE YOURSELF IN THE
RACE CONVERSATION**

*That's not a chip on my shoulder.
That's your foot on my neck.*

—MALCOLM X

WAYNE FRANCIS

My *heart* stopped when I saw the sirens in my rearview mirror. In a moment of terror, I realized I had forgotten to turn my lights on, and what started as a fun-filled, carefree night out quickly turned south.

Jimmy Rollins is one of my favorite people in the world. He is a fellow pastor who leads a large church in Baltimore and shares my love for food and fun. A few months ago, he was in town visiting with his daughter, so one night, I took them out to Tredici, one of my favorite Italian restaurants. Tredici is in a neighborhood called Purchase, which, if you can't tell from the name, is one of those upscale, country-club-type places where every other car is a Maserati.

We were the only Black people in the entire place, and we shut it down. When Jimmy and I get to talking, we have a habit of closing out the restaurant. By the time we got the check, it was 11 p.m. We said thank you, got in our car, took a left out of the parking lot, and had barely picked out our playlist before the lights came on.

That's a scary moment for anyone, but for three Black people rolling through a predominantly White neighborhood late at night—let's just say I got those underarm itches. I was trying to take deep breaths while Jimmy was machine-gunning the devil, praying prayers I couldn't understand in the name of Jesus. Between prayers, he kept telling his daughter to stay calm and silent in the back seat. Thinking back, she was the calmest one in the car.

Like me, Jimmy is a Black man. Unlike me, Jimmy is a big ol' brother. He ain't a Prius or a Mini Cooper; he's what we call a "Big Body Benz" on the streets. 7 Series. Full suspension. The type that hugs the road nice and tight. Although he is the nicest man in the world, at first glance, he is intimidating.

The Spirit was moving in the car, and Jimmy was sinking into his seat, trying to look as least threatening as he could. We were grown men, thinking this could go either way. The officer knocked on my window, shining his flashlight in my face. My hands formed fists as I nervously clenched the steering wheel at 10 and 2 and asked if I could roll my window down. For those of you who don't know, 10 and 2 is the position you put your hands on the wheel when being pulled over by the police. If you are a person of color, you are very familiar with it, because you know it aids in creating a deescalated atmosphere.

"What are you doing here?" he asked, not even letting me get my window down before asking the question on his mind. Typically, the first question is "Do you know why I pulled you over?" But apparently, the more pressing matter was to know what business three Black people had driving around Purchase.

Here's the thing: we were eating at that restaurant because it's my spot. It's like an episode of *Cheers* every time I walk into Tredici; everyone knows my name. We were in that neighborhood because I live down the road. Granted, my square footage may not be quite as extensive as that of the houses right by the restaurant, but those are my people; I pastor a church right down the road.

But maybe he didn't believe me because he asked for my ID and registration.

That hurt. It wasn't so much what he was saying. It was how he was saying it. The tone was condescending, like a parent telling a child they are in trouble. My ego was trying to flare up, but I wouldn't let it. Instead, I once again asked permission to slowly reach into my glove box to grab the items he requested. If that sounds like overkill to you, it's not. Sadly, many Black people have to employ these tactics, regardless of their socioeconomic status. Every movement matters, so every movement is methodical.

The cop took my license and registration back to his car, and that's when the sweat started dripping. Jimmy leaned over to me, like two kids sitting in the back of a classroom.

"Bro, you got that registration in order, right?" he whispered. "Inspection and all? What if he asks you to get out of the car? What's your plan?"

I couldn't breathe.

Honestly, I didn't even know my rights. I wasn't sure what I would do if the cop asked me to step out of the vehicle. My only goal was to deescalate at all costs. Don't cause any trouble. Don't add to the aggression. Don't move too fast, don't say the wrong thing. It was a stressful moment.

All because I hadn't turned on my headlights.

When the cop realized I was telling the truth, he returned to the car, handed me my things, politely reminded me my lights were off, and sent us on our way.

As the cop drove off, the car was silent (and that is saying something for Jimmy and me). A routine stop had turned into an anxiety-ridden experience. After all, Jimmy's daughter was in the car, and we've both seen viral videos of how that can go.

The cop took one look at us and decided we didn't belong in that neighborhood. I don't know if you've ever had that happen to you, but it's disheartening. In the cop's mind, we were up to no good. The tone in his voice indicated we better have a good reason for being there. We were in my own community, around my neighbors, the place where I have the most influence. And yet, the cop treated me like an elementary student out in the hallway without a hall pass.

That is profiling.

That is suffocating.

That is stifling.

That feels like a knee holding you down.

Unless you've had your head buried in the sand for the past decade, you've heard about stories of profiling that have ended much worse. As uncomfortable as these stories are, we must take time to not only talk about them but allow ourselves to *feel* the sadness, confusion, and pain that these injustices cause. If we keep glossing over tragedies, we'll keep repeating them. So whether you are hearing these stories for the first time or the hundredth time, take the time to *feel* the weight of them.

Just a Jog

On February 23, 2020, Ahmaud Arbery, a twenty-five-year-old Black man, went for a jog in his neighborhood. During his run, he stopped by a house under construction; moments later, he was shot and killed by a father and son duo named Gregory and Travis McMichael.

Allegedly, there had been a series of break-ins in that neighborhood, and Arbery fit the suspect's description, so when the McMichaels spotted him out for a run, they decided to act. However, the police have no reports of those break-ins.

With generational racism flowing through their veins and two guns in their truck, they chased Arbery down and confronted him. When they stepped out of their vehicle, things escalated quickly and ended with Arbery lying dead in the street, one bullet in his hand, and two in his chest.

Arbery was unarmed and had no stolen possessions on him, but the McMichaels took one look at him and decided he was a thief. That's profiling. How many White people had jogged through the very same neighborhood that day? No one thought anything of it, but Arbery was different. Why? Because there is a narrative that Black men are thieves and threats.

For the next two and a half months, nothing happened. The two men slept in their own beds while Arbery's body lay in the ground. It wasn't until there was a public outcry that any measure of justice took place.

I remember texting John right after the story came out and telling him how hard it was to watch. Arbery's death hit a little different for me because I run through my neighborhood every week (okay, almost every week). And I hold my giant phone in my hand. What if someone who looks like me commits a crime while I'm out on my next jog? All it would take is one angry, confused, or radical person, and I'm done. That type of thought will mess with you, especially when you have children at home.

"I Can't Breathe"

A few months after Arbery's murder, a forty-six-year-old Black man named George Floyd was sitting in his car outside of Cup Foods, a convenience store in Minneapolis. Police officers knocked on his window, responding to a call that Floyd had tried to use a counterfeit twenty-dollar bill to pay for cigarettes. Floyd was terrified. He was trying to catch his breath and get his hands on the steering wheel, but within seconds, the White police officer Derek Chauvin already had his gun drawn.

Floyd repeatedly begged the officer not to shoot and struggled to get his wits about him, so the officer asked him to get out of the car. What followed was an intense and disturbing series of events that eventually led to Floyd lying on the ground with the officer's knee pressed against his neck.

For seven minutes and forty-six seconds.*

"I can't breathe," Floyd told Chauvin more than twenty

---

* It was originally documented at eight minutes and forty-six seconds, and the *New York Times* notes that the time is "no longer exact" (https://www .nytimes.com/2020/06/18/us/george-floyd-timing.html). But whatever the official time was, it was that many minutes and seconds too long.

times as he begged for his life. But the officer didn't let up. He didn't even uncuff him. Floyd tried to refer to him as "Sir," and then "Mr. Officer," but the man was not listening.

He held him down as if he were no more than a piece of meat, and Floyd was dead within the hour.

A call about a counterfeit twenty-dollar bill escalated into a deadly encounter. George Floyd, a man, created in the image of God, was reduced to something much less.

Racism is real, and profiling is a problem because it reduces humans to stereotypes. I'm not saying crimes should not be punished; all responsible people agree there should be penalties for breaking the law. All I'm saying is if a Black person commits a crime, that person deserves the right to stand trial and be treated like a human being rather than killed in the street.

Heart Check

If you are a person of color, I'm sure you could fill this chapter with your stories. These stories probably trigger some memories for you, because for every tragic ending, there are several other events that could've ended just as poorly. It's a real thing, and it's terrifying.

But the question is, What is going on in your *heart* while you read these stories? No matter what color your skin is, what is your *heart* saying? What emotions are you feeling?

Apathetic?

Angry?

Hopeless?

Feel the Burn

———

Paul Brand was a twentieth-century doctor who spent years living and working with people who had leprosy (also called Hansen's disease), devoting his life to eradicating the disease. One of the terrible things about the disease is that it numbs your nervous system. Slowly but surely, you lose feeling in your limbs, and before you know it, you can't feel any pain or other sensation in your extremities. Many people with the disease lost limbs because they couldn't feel the damage they were doing to themselves until it was too late.

The pain of profiling can have a similar effect. If you've been surrounded by or the victim of racism for years, there is a good chance you've learned to go numb. Apathy is one of the ways your body copes with pain. When the pain gets too bad, it shuts off your feelings and helps you go numb. Not in a literal sense, like leprosy, but anyone who has ever had a season of apathy knows how real it seems.

Aware of this danger in his own life, Dr. Brand developed a routine. After a long, hard day of being in close proximity with leprosy, he would fill up a bucket with scalding hot water and immerse his hands in it. It was painful every time, and that was the point. As long as he could feel the burn, he knew he hadn't contracted the disease.

In the Bible, leprosy is a metaphor for sin, and if you are around the sin of racism all the time, check in with your *heart* to make sure you haven't grown numb. Pain and bitterness have a subtle way of convincing us not to care about anything, but we can't let that happen. Like Dr. Brand, we have to learn to check in and make sure we can still feel.

Do you still feel something when you read these stories?

Pain? Confusion? Sadness? Fear? Anything? As much as it hurts, the pain is a gift. It means apathy hasn't won the battle. You are still alive.

And if you answered no to that question, maybe this chapter has revealed that your heart has grown hard. That may be difficult to hear, but remember: awareness is always a gift because now you can see the problem at hand.

Holocaust survivor Elie Wiesel once said, "The opposite of love is not hate, it's indifference." He was a man who knew something about pain. His stories about surviving the Holocaust are brutal, and although he continued to carry the pain with him, he didn't let apathy win. The fact that he was still alive was a miracle, so he decided to give the rest of his life to love, not indifference.

These days, it's all too easy to go numb, and there are plenty of substances that will gladly help you do it. But don't let yourself stop caring. Honestly, I would rather you be passionate about something I disagree with than apathetic. The second you find yourself buying in to the famous Bruce Hornsby chorus (or in my case the Tupac sample), "That's just the way it is / Some things will never change," it's time to take a play out of Dr. Brand's playbook. No, I'm not telling you to dip your hand in scalding hot water; I'm telling you to get around people who have stories of profiling. Listen to them, and allow yourself to tune in to their emotional pain.

Feel the burn!

If you don't have any friends who fit that category, that's a whole other issue that we tackle in Part Three. For now, just turn on a movie about or read a biography of a person of color who has experienced persecution.

Let yourself cry.

Let yourself get angry.

Let yourself feel confused.

Any emotion is better than apathy. The pain is real—your job is to let yourself enter in and feel it. And if you are feeling really bold, ask the Spirit to help you feel again. Here's one of the most dangerously beautiful prayers you can ever pray: *Lord, would you break my heart for what breaks yours?*

Pull Back Over

After the cop drove off that night, I got angry. The day I moved into Westchester County, I felt like I had made it. For a Black man like me to come from where I did, it was an accomplishment I was proud of. But when a cop questions whether you should be there, it makes you feel like you still don't belong.

Any time a celebrity like Lebron James has something to say, watch how quickly people complain about a millionaire whining. But you have to understand: it feels like there is a glass ceiling that no amount of money or success can break for some Black people. No matter how far we rise, we feel like we can't be equal.

I don't know what the cop's motives were, but I know what I heard. I heard a man who was trying to pull the rug out from under me. And it was frustrating because if he had just handled it with a different tone, I wouldn't be writing about it today. I understand that I forgot to flip on my headlights. He could've just asked to see my registration and sent me on my way. Instead, he questioned whether or not we belonged in that part of town.

When I tried to get back on the road, it wasn't happening. My body was shaking too much to drive, so I pulled over, my hands still clenched to the wheel, and the venting began. Jimmy and I sat there for a while, talking about how the cop's tone had ruined a great night and how frustrating and unnecessary the whole thing had been.

We let ourselves feel the anger for a while, and it helped.

Sometimes the best thing to do after you get pulled over is to pull back over. Anger is a real emotion, and if we keep it bottled up, it can turn nasty. If we don't find ways to replenish, we will look for ways to retaliate. That venting session didn't fix everything. Honestly, I still carry some pain around from that night. But it did help us leave the anger in the car instead of taking it home.

Thank God Jimmy and I had that conversation. The cop may have ruined our night, but that doesn't mean we had to let him ruin anyone else's. The anger may be justified, but we have an opportunity to direct it to the proper place.

Do all the stories of profiling make you want to start throwing punches?

One practical way to *feel the burn* is to let yourself get angry. Maybe something is welling up inside of you that you can't control or explain—a deeply rooted anger you've always had but never felt permission to express. Let me give you permission to feel that anger in a healthy setting, around the right people whom you trust. The anger is looking for an escape, a place to go. If you stuff it back down, it will wreak havoc, like an unwanted houseguest in your *heart*. Let it go. Give it space to run free. But do it in a way that you aren't going to regret the next day.

The Book We Never Talk About

Although there are sixty-six books in the Bible, some of them don't get much airtime. Lamentations is one of those books that gets lost among all the prophets at the end of the Old Testament. The Israelites experienced a terrible season of exile in Babylon, so the author writes five poems remembering and reflecting on how difficult the journey was. It's an entire book dedicated to the art of mourning.

If the stories in this chapter made you feel hopeless, remember that it's okay to mourn. Passages of lament are in the Bible because God wants us to lament. When we are lamenting, it's easy to feel like no one else understands what we are going through, but scripture reminds us we are in good company and invites us to process our pain and even get angry with God.

We aren't very good at this. These days, hopelessness is almost taboo. And sometimes pastors can be the worst of all. After all, the word *gospel* means good news; plus, people get bad news thrown at them all week, so on Sunday, we want to give them some hope. But the only way to let go of our pain is to lament, so unless we want to carry it around with us everywhere we go, we have to mourn.

If you feel hopeless reading this chapter, resist the urge to speed past the mourning process. It's okay to be sad for a time. Feel it, mourn, and let the sadness run its course, because "weeping may stay for the night, / but rejoicing comes in the morning" (Ps. 30:5).

In Every Way

When Jimmy and I pulled over, I was upset. Nobody likes feeling like an outsider in their hometown. Part of me was hopeless. I was thinking, *If this is still happening to me even after all the work I've put in, maybe it's just my lot in life.* Part of me was furious and wanted to make a scene. And another part of me wanted to find a way to numb the pain and pretend the night had never happened. Because what many Black readers can attest to is the fact that I could've filled this chapter with thousands of pages of examples of the pain profiling has caused.

One of the scariest parts about COVID-19 in the beginning was that we didn't have enough ventilators for everyone who needed them. Since the virus often made it difficult for patients to breathe on their own, doctors intubated those in need, so the ventilator could pump fresh air and oxygen into their airways.

As a nation, it feels like a tube needs to be inserted into our institutions to pump life-enhancing air into the lungs of Black Americans. Like the denial of oxygen, the deprivation of equal opportunities asphyxiates people of color. Equal opportunities aren't just essential; they are a life force. When you feel like you are suffocating in hopelessness because you don't have access to the same trajectory your White peers do, it's not long before you feel light-headed and incapacitated.

Imagine gasping for air every time your ten-year-old leaves the house in the morning because you are worried about what may happen if they have a run-in with law enforcement. Imagine nearly hyperventilating every time you get a phone call from your son's school because you are worried he was on the wrong side of a crime committed by other young Black men.

We can't breathe.

When we get pulled over, we can't breathe.

When we walk through predominantly White neighborhoods, we can't breathe.

We want to take a deep breath, but sometimes it feels like all we can do is inhale centuries of demeaning pollution and death. We need some help breathing. But let's be honest, a ventilator is a temporary fix; we can't have open-handed conversations with tubes down our throats. What we really need is a cure.

Racism is a pandemic that needs more than a ventilator; it needs a vaccine.

It's tempting to make a mad dash in search of some huge solution. But as Jimmy often reminds me, the antidote to racism is the gospel.

One of my favorite parts about the gospel story is the path Jesus was willing to take to get to the cross. The resurrection is the foundation of our faith, and we celebrate it every chance we get, but let's not overlook all Jesus was willing to walk through to get there. The writer of Hebrews says it this way: "For we do not have a high priest who is unable to empathize with our weaknesses, but we have one who has been *tempted in every way*, just as we are—yet he did not sin" (Heb. 4:15, emphasis added).

If you are feeling overwhelmed reading this chapter, remember that Jesus knows the feeling. The night he was arrested, he was so stressed out he was sweating blood. If a moment of racism has made you feel all alone, remember that Jesus's best friends left him hanging in his moment of need. If a moment of profiling has left you feeling betrayed, remember that Judas, a guy who walked with Jesus for years, turned him in to the authorities. And if you feel hopeless right now, remember that Jesus felt the same way while he was hanging on a cross, unable to breathe.

Pain.

Stress.

Betrayal.

Confusion.

Death.

Jesus experienced it all.

He knows how you feel.

That doesn't fix your situation, and I don't mean it to. I say that to be an encouragement as you continue forward. Jimmy gave me space to process my pain in the car, and the longer I talked, the better I felt. It didn't fix everything, but knowing someone was in it with me helped me make sense of the pain. It seems like solidarity was a huge part of Jesus's mission. Yes, he came to defeat sin and death, but he also came to sit in the middle of our pain with us.

After a while, I even started to sympathize a bit with the police officer. No matter who you are, pulling someone over at 11 p.m. must be scary. After all, he had his own life and his own family to think about. Many cops have lost their lives while protecting and serving.

Maybe that's why Jesus told us to pray for the people who persecute us (Matt. 5:44). When we pray for them—and I mean really pray for their well-being, not just that God heap judgment on them—it forces us to put ourselves in their shoes.

I may not agree with what the cop did, but I can seek to understand it. And the only way to get there is by trusting the process instead of shoving down feelings.

Humans have an innate ability to cope with pain. God made us that way. But when we keep our guard *up*, the walls won't fall *down*. We have to be willing to *feel the burn* together. Jimmy felt it for me, and I felt it for him. We carried it for each other because life change happens when we trust each other enough to process pain together.

I could've shut down my emotions and let the anger eat at me.

I could've gotten angry and created even more problems for myself.

I could've called it quits, sold my car, and resolved to never drive again.

But it's like my mother told me all those years ago, *Jus' keep walkin', babee.*

Eventually, I looked at Jimmy, and he nodded. I realized I still hadn't rolled my window back up from the interaction with the officer because my hands were still clenched tightly to my steering wheel. I took a few deep breaths and felt the oxygen flow through my lungs and into my body. As I enjoyed breathing deeply again, I let go of my steering wheel, noticed how sore my hands were, made sure my lights were on, and got back on the road.

Check Your Posture

LET'S TALK ABOUT WHITE PRIVILEGE

To refuse to listen to someone's cries for justice and equality
until the request comes in a language you feel comfortable
with is a way of asserting your dominance over them.

—IJEOMA OLUO

JOHN SIEBELING

It's time to talk about White privilege. If that is an uncomfortable or even repulsive sentence for you to read, you're not alone. This is a tough subject for a lot of White people, including me. Privilege may be uncomfortable to talk about, but it's foundational for learning how to have conversations about race, so please resist the urge to skip this chapter and keep a soft *heart* while reading it.

In 2002, the original Spider-Man hit the theaters. You remember—that one with Tobey Maguire, right? Leslie and I went to see it, and at the time, that was a big deal for us. We had two young kids at home and rarely had any time for ourselves. The movie didn't start until 9 p.m., and the theater was packed, but we managed to grab two seats in the back and sat down just as the trailers began.

An African American family, who had brought their young daughter with them, was sitting three rows in front of us. She was about the same age as our daughter, and Leslie admits she noticed them because she wondered why they would let their daughter stay out so late.

But as the credits rolled, Leslie had a moment she still remembers all these years later. As the family stood to leave, she watched the little girl swing a Disney princess backpack around her shoulder. The backpack had pictures of four princesses, and each one of them was White. Suddenly, she had a realization.

"She doesn't even have a princess," she whispered, tears starting to fill her eyes as she elbowed me in the side. But my mind was too far off in the Marvel world to understand what she was saying. She motioned over to the little girl and tried again. "Why is every princess on her backpack White?"

For the past few decades, Leslie and I have had an increasing awareness of the reality that our nation is, in many ways, skewed in favor of White people—even something as small as our daughter growing up with Disney princesses who look like her.

During one of the seasons of my life when I was trying to learn more about White privilege, I picked up a book called *White Picket Fences: Turning Toward Love in a World Divided by Privilege* by Amy Julia Becker. In it, she tells the heartfelt story of her journey toward coming to see and understand her White privilege, and I resonated with her words at a deep level. The reason we felt like the color of our skin was giving us a head start in life was because it was.

White privilege can be defined as "inherent advantages possessed by a White person on the basis of their race in a society characterized by racial inequality and injustice."[1] In other words, if you are White and live in the United States, you've enjoyed certain advantages throughout your life that you didn't have to earn.

Does that mean your life has been easy? No.

Does that mean you haven't worked hard for the things you have? No.

Does that mean you've never experienced poverty, persecution, or problems? No.

White privilege doesn't mean you haven't had any problems; it means your skin color hasn't been one of them. You don't have to consider how your skin color will impact your day-to-day, minute-to-minute life. When I say it's time to talk about White privilege, I'm not saying we're going to shame you for being White or invalidate your life experiences or devalue your accomplishments. But I am saying that White readers have to understand a very real reality if they have any chance of empathizing with a person of color in a conversation.

During my journey toward seeing, understanding, and acknowledging White privilege, I've learned two things. The first is that being White is not my fault; the second is that being White has given me an advantage. On the one hand, I shouldn't feel bad for my ethnicity; shame doesn't move the race conversation forward. But on the other hand, I've been given an advantage, and it is my responsibility to do something productive with what I have.

Check Your Privilege

At this point, you may be asking, *John, what do you mean by "advantage"?*

This exercise may help. Kenya Bundy, a caterer from Richmond, Virginia, recently created a "check your privilege" challenge. One day, while sitting in her car, she scribbled down a list of twelve negative things she has experienced as a Black woman. Curious to see whether others had experienced something similar, she turned it into a challenge that went viral on social media.[2] In the video, she encourages you to raise all ten fingers and then put a finger down for every item that applies to your life.

Let's try it. Put your coffee down and put ten fingers up in the air:

* Put a finger down if you have been called a racial slur.

* Put a finger down if you have been followed in a store unnecessarily.

* Put a finger down if someone has crossed the street to avoid passing you.

* Put a finger down if someone has clenched their purse in an elevator with you.

* Put a finger down if someone has stepped off of an elevator to keep from riding with you.

* Put a finger down if you have been accused of not being able to afford something expensive.

* Put a finger down if you have had fear in your heart when stopped by the police.

* Put a finger down if you have never been given a pass on a citation that you deserved.

* Put a finger down if you have been stopped or detained by police for no valid reason.

* Put a finger down if you have been bullied solely because of your race.

* Put a finger down if you have been denied service solely because of the color of your skin.

* Put a finger down if you have ever had to teach your children how not to get killed by the police.

How many of your fingers are still up in the air?

If you don't have kids or carry a purse, two of those items don't apply to you, but you get the point. Recently Wayne and I did this exercise together, and by the end of it, I still had nine fingers in the air, and Wayne had only two. And to be honest, the reason I didn't have all ten in the air is that I once wandered into an upscale store one afternoon on vacation while wearing a T-shirt and shorts. Meanwhile, Wayne was across the table asking for a straw to finish drinking his flat white because he was barely holding on to the two fingers he had left.

I got curious and did this exercise with several Black and White people on our staff, and the pattern was very telling. Every White person still had two hands with fingers up, while every Black person was down to a single hand.

That's privilege.

Now, some White people in the world could put all their fingers down during that exercise, and if you are one of them, this concept may be difficult for you to accept. But try to take a step back and see the bigger picture. By and large, White people do not have to deal with as many stereotypes or overcome as many obstacles as Black people. That is privilege. And if you want to engage in open-handed conversations about *God and race*, you have to see it and seek to understand it. If you can't acknowledge White privilege, I personally believe you are making it difficult for yourself to engage in conversations with people of color. However, when you do acknowledge it, suddenly all sorts of carefully constructed walls begin to fall.

American History

I recently looked at a picture of my fifth-grade class and was a little shocked to remember just how White my school was. I mean, one of the girls had a pretty good tan at the time, but there wasn't a single person of color in the entire class. Remember, I grew up in a predominantly White neighborhood called Westminster in Baton Rouge, Louisiana. There were only a few Black kids in the entire school. But I never thought anything of it. I was much more concerned with playing soccer at recess and what snack we were going to have afterward.

(By the way, one of the other kids in that class was a girl named Leslie; at the time, we had no idea we'd be spending the rest of our lives together.)

Every afternoon, when we got back from playing soccer in the Louisiana heat, we'd sit down and learn about history. Our young minds were ready to absorb whatever information our American history textbooks presented. It wasn't until decades later that I realized we might not have been getting the whole truth.

The primary way most Americans learn about events that happened hundreds of years ago is by relying on other people's accounts. What we believe about our history is shaped by the teachers we've had and the books we've read. Very few people shape their account of history by going back and reading primary sources—firsthand accounts, historical documents, and so forth. We read (and are taught) summarized, highly abridged versions of history that give us overviews, highlights, and main facts. But one of the things we need to remember about privilege is that those who have it control much of what gets taught. As the old saying goes, "History is written by the victors."

So let's take a dive back into the history books and revisit a few key moments together.

The Three-Fifths Compromise

One of the big questions our young country was wrestling with while writing the Constitution in 1787 was how much pull each state should have when making countrywide decisions. Since some states were already much larger than others, the members of the Constitutional Convention decided to base representation on population. But that brought up another question: *Should enslaved people be counted as people or property?*

The South had a vested interest in counting slaves as people because it would give the White landowners more power to push decisions through. Ironically, counting slaves as people would provide their White owners with the power to continue treating them like property. The South wanted to have their cake and eat it too.

Do you see the dilemma?

Eventually, the North and the South reached a compromise. They decided one slave would count as three-fifths of a person. While this compromise was strategic on the part of the North and ultimately aided in abolishing slavery, it highlighted a terrible reality in our country: we saw enslaved Black people as being less than fully human.

I'll be honest, I don't remember learning a lot of that in my history class.

In *White Picket Fences*, Becker talks about growing up in the Inner Banks of North Carolina, within walking distance of a plantation. Yet she didn't learn the full story of slavery. She grew up hearing that slaves were really good at working with cotton and were putting in hard work to help bring prosperity to the South—as if they were co-workers who were benefiting from all the success. Hardly an accurate picture of slavery.[3]

The United States was founded on Christian principles, but are you willing to also acknowledge that while a basic tenet of the Christian faith says humans are all created in God's image, we believed that was only three-fifths true about our Black brothers and sisters?

The Open Casket That Opened Our Eyes

Emmett Till grew up on the South Side of Chicago. He was born in 1941 and raised by a single mother named Mamie Till. One day in 1955 Mamie dropped Emmett at the Sixty-Third Street train station, where he boarded a train to Mississippi to visit his cousins. That was the last time she ever saw her only child alive.

While in Mississippi, fourteen-year-old Till went into a market and flirted with the cashier, a twenty-one-year-old White woman named Carolyn Bryant, who was married to the shop owner.[4] Four days later, Bryant's relatives—allegedly just her husband, Roy, and his half brother J. W. Milam—kidnapped Till in the middle of the night. They brutally beat and tortured the boy, shot him in the head, and then threw his mutilated body into the Tallahatchie River. The body was discovered three days later, so beaten and maimed that it was almost impossible to identify.

The jury for the case was all-White and all-male. Bryant and Milam never even bothered to take the stand to explain themselves. Carolyn testified that Emmett had grabbed and tried to rape her (although more than sixty years later, she admitted that what she said on the stand was not true). In his closing remarks, Sidney Carlton, their defense attorney, told the jury, "Your ancestors will turn over in their grave" if they didn't acquit the two men and added, "I'm sure every last Anglo-Saxon one of you has the courage to free these men."[5]

What was the all-White jury's verdict? Not guilty.

When Mamie Till received the body of her son, she couldn't even recognize him: "At first glance, the body didn't seem to be human."[6] She decided she had to act, so she held a five-day open-casket funeral for her son. Thousands of people came. Soon the story got the attention of the press and spread throughout the nation.

As an entire race mourned the tragic and horrific murder of Emmett Till, anger began to rise. The boy's disfigured body on display for all to see was a breaking point. One hundred days later, Rosa Parks, inspired by the courage of Mamie Till, refused to give up her seat on a bus and was arrested for violating segregation laws, and the civil rights movement was off to the races.

Oftentimes the people who have never heard of Emmett Till are the same ones who struggle to understand why Black people take a stand and protest. Recently a telling meme was making its way around the internet: "Crazy thing is, they think all of this is about George Floyd when we're still crying tears for Emmett Till."[7]

Educator and activist Jose Del Barrio says, "White privilege is your history being part of the core curriculum and mine being taught as an elective."[8] If the only history we learn is limited in scope—predominantly anemic on the subject of slavery and glossing over the impact of the Jim Crow era—how can we accurately learn to empathize with the pain of a people group?

The people who *write* history now have the responsibility to *right* these wrongs.

A Crack in the Foundation

We could go on and on with historical examples, and with other groups of people who have been oppressed throughout

American history, but that's well beyond the scope of this book. The point is, our nation's history may not be as neat and tidy as you think—and you may not know it as well as you thought you did. An entire group of people has collectively suffered more than four hundred years of pain at the hands of White people and a system designed to favor them.

The only way for there to be true freedom and equality for everyone in our nation—not just on paper, but in practice—is to confront that history and acknowledge the privilege White people have exercised.

In his famous "Letter from a Birmingham Jail," Dr. King wrote, "Like a boil that can never be cured so long as it is covered up but must be opened with all its ugliness to the natural medicines of air and light, injustice must be exposed."[9] We can't move forward until we are willing to look back at the past, and the truth is, our history is darker than we care to admit.

We have a crack in our foundation. For more than four hundred years, the system we built has created privilege for one ethnicity and pain for others. The race hasn't been fair. White people have by and large had a massive head start.

If you've ever built anything, you know how important the foundation is. When there is a crack at the base, all it takes is a little pressure for the whole thing to collapse. We've seen this happen several times throughout our history. From Red Summer in 1919 to the civil rights movement in the 1960s to the protests of 2020, all it takes is a little pressure to reveal just how shaky the foundation is. If you are White, there are two different ways to approach those types of moments.

The White-knuckle approach is to get angry and ask, *Why can't they get over it already?*

The open-handed approach is to empathize and ask, *What is broken in the system that is causing all this pain to spill over? Where did we go wrong, and how can we course-correct for the future?*

Central Park Privilege

You may remember the case in 2020 when Christian Cooper, a Black man, asked Amy Cooper, a White woman (no relation), to leash her dog in Central Park. They were in a popular section of New York City's famed park, renowned for excellent bird watching, and dogs are disruptive to birds that rest and nest there. Although his tone was civil and respectful, she was offended by the courteous request and let him know it. Then Christian started filming the interaction with his phone. Disheveled and angry, Amy asked him to stop filming, and when he declined, she became irate. She showed her privilege by calling the police and telling them that she was being threatened by an African American man in Central Park and that she needed police aid right away, inflecting her voice to make it sound like she was in real danger.

Wayne joked with me once that any Black man who is bird watching is likely not a threat. He's from New York City and says the only birds he watches are pigeons eating leftover pizza crusts on his dash toward the subway.

But what's no laughing matter is the fact that Black men have been unequivocally characterized as immediate threats. As many of our Black brothers and sisters march through the streets, one of the popular slogans on signs, T-shirts, and sweatshirts is "Hands up, don't shoot." That slogan comes from the commonly understood position of surrender. However, it took on a new light after the shooting of Michael Brown on August 9, 2014, in Ferguson, Missouri. Though there is a dispute over whether or not he said those words before he was shot by the police officer, the message is clear: privilege can cause you to perceive even open hands as a threat from minorities.

Amy Cooper and Christian Cooper live in the same world but were handed different sets of rules.

Amy Cooper, a White woman.

Christian Cooper, a Black man.

Same last name; two different realities based on skin color. One with privilege, the other without. The truth is, things could have ended very badly for Christian that day.[10]

Whether you want to see and acknowledge that or not, the truth is, empathizing with the problems privilege causes is a prerequisite for having open-handed conversations about race.

Heart Check

I just threw a lot at you. But remember what we are trying to accomplish in this part of the book. You ask God to search your *heart* to "see if there is any offensive way in me, / and lead me in the way everlasting" (Ps. 139:24).

What is going on in your heart as you read this chapter?

Have you found yourself getting defensive or angry?

Are your fists clenched?

How white are your knuckles?

If I'm talking to you right now, don't ignore those feelings; they are telling. If you are getting defensive, it may be because there are some offensive ways in you, and God is trying to lead you in the way everlasting. Don't you hate it when God answers our prayers like that? Lean in. I know that's scary, and probably a little painful, but the fruit is worth the fight.

Everyone who knows me (or has listened to more than one of my sermons) knows how much I hate working out. I despise it. It's never come naturally to me. But as much as I hate working out, I love the results. I have come to understand the importance of pushing through the pain.

Letting God work to expose the things hidden in our *hearts* is not comfortable, but remember that the Lord disciplines those he loves, so like me at the gym, let's push through the pain and enjoy the results on the other side. Here are two questions to ask yourself.

Am I Seeking to See, Acknowledge, and Understand My Privilege?

I'm amazed when I talk to friends who push back on privilege. There's a saying about privilege: "Some people are born on third base and go through life thinking they hit a triple."[11]

Is there a chance that's you?

If you want to have productive, open-handed conversations with someone of a different race, few things will move the needle more than acknowledging your privilege. And even if you aren't ready to recognize your privilege, start with acknowledging the collective advantage White people have had over the past four hundred years.

Call up a friend who is a person of color and ask them to explain White privilege to you in their own words. Ask them if they've seen ways you have benefited from privilege and invite them to continue pointing it out to you as you go.

Can you see it? Because you can't talk about something that you can't see.

Can you acknowledge it? Because you won't get anywhere if you won't accept it.

And are you seeking to understand it more? Because there is always more to learn.

Am I Using My Privilege to Reach Back and Help Others Up?

If you go throughout your day today feeling bad because of the color of your skin, you've missed the point. Shame is not helpful; action is. Learning to empathize with someone who doesn't look like you and gaining some perspective goes a long way.

Once you see and acknowledge your privilege, it's time to start doing something productive with what you have. Anyone who has privilege (of any kind) also has a responsibility to use that privilege for good. If you are White, you have an excellent opportunity to move things forward and bring awareness. Speak up! Instead of using your privilege to try to push yourself forward, use it to reach back and pull others up. As former British prime minister Benjamin Disraeli said, "Justice is truth in action."

Check Your Posture

———————

At the beginning of this chapter we checked our *privilege*; now that we've talked through the implications of all these stories, let's check our *heart posture*.

Raise your hands in front of you again. This time clench your fists with all your fingers down. Think about the illustration we went through earlier. A disparity exists. You may not identify with the rallying cry of "hands up, don't shoot" and the plight of inner-city Black people, but I hope you can identify what we need at this time: *the universal posture of surrender.*

This time, raise one finger for each of these biblical truths you are ready to affirm to be true about yourself and *every* human being:

* I am made in the image of God (Gen. 1:27).

* I am fearfully and wonderfully made (Ps. 139:14).

* I am on this earth for a reason (Eph. 2:10).

* All people deserve my respect (Matt. 7:12).

* All skin hues are precious in God's sight (Rev. 7:9).

* I am called to love my neighbor as myself (Matt. 22:39).

* Every person I meet is my neighbor (Luke 10:36).

* Silence is not enough; it's time for me to speak up (Prov. 31:8).

* Love is not just words or speech but action (1 John 3:17).

* I am willing to lay down my life for others (1 John 3:16).

If you have all ten fingers up, congratulations—you're in a position of surrender. If you don't, no judgment. It just means you have more work to do. Remember, it's not about perfection; it's about progress. And don't worry, this is a tough subject, and we are all in the same boat, working through our past problems and prejudice to open our hands and move forward toward racial healing.

Forgive, Don't Forget

WAYNE FRANCIS

When I was in Bible School, my best friend was a White guy from the Midwest named Joe. At the end of our first year, I invited him to spend the summer in the Bronx. He didn't have anything else going on, so he took me up on the offer. Who wouldn't want to spend their summer in New York?

Our only plan for those three months was to make some money so we could afford to go back to school in the fall. Books and school fees weren't cheap, and at some point, I was going to need to buy a second suit. At Bible School, we had to wear a shirt and tie every day, and then put them back on to preach at revivals four nights a week. When you have only one suit, it's not easy to keep it looking fresh. I always hung it up in the bathroom while I took extra hot showers; I pressed that thing so many times it felt like silk.

We needed a job, and we needed it fast. But we had only one car, so we were willing to do anything as long as it was together.

My older sister landed us a job at a large investment advising firm. Before you start wondering how two first-year Bible students got that kind of job, let me clarify that statement: she landed us a job in the *mailroom* of a large investment advising firm. Every morning we got to walk into the main floor, with all the windows and natural light, but we didn't get to stay there. Instead, we would head to the second floor and journey back to the mailroom, tucked away from the offices.

Although it was not overtly said, the mailroom had that "minimum-wagers-abide-here" feeling. Besides Joe, there was only one other White person in the entire place—some Italian guy. But we all worked hard, sorting thousands of pieces of mail every day. C-suite execs would rush by all the time, seemingly always running behind schedule, and throw us packages that needed to be shipped overnight to investors. And most of the day was devoted to cleaning out the mail chute because letters were always getting stuck. Once we finally jiggled them free, we'd load them onto our carts and walk around delivering the mail to all the cubicles.

It wasn't glamorous, but we were there for the money. It wasn't like we were looking to climb the corporate ladder, but two weeks in, the day we brought home our very first paychecks, it all felt worth it. We grabbed our checks and rushed out the door, licking our chops, ready to open them up and finally have a few dollars in our pockets so we could hit the town. I was eager to swap the Men's Wearhouse suit I rocked my first year for an upgrade from Reiss, a popular store in SoHo at the time. It was time to level up from that polyester blend to some fine wool.

"We've worked eighty hours now," Joe said on the drive home. "Multiply that by $11.50, and this is going to be big for us."

"Wait, wait, wait," I said, interrupting him. "What did you just say? How much are you getting paid?"

"$11.50."

"Bro, I'm only making $10."

I was so mad. It's not like Joe was majoring in "Mail Sorting" at school. We had the exact same credentials (none), we applied the same day, for the same job, in my hometown. Plus, my sister was the one who got him the position in the first place. I sat back in frustration and started wondering what that Italian guy was making.

Apparently, at that company, being White got you an immediate $1.50 raise.

If you've never experienced being treated less-than for the color of your skin, it's tough to explain how bad it hurts. It wasn't the money; it was the message. It's belittling when someone tells you that you are worth less than another person, for a simple job. We weren't doing brain surgery; we were sorting mail.

Moments like that leave a mark. At some deep level, the world told me I was less than my White counterpart, that my time wasn't quite as valuable as his. To make it worse, Joe just sort of shrugged it off. He wasn't mean about it or anything, but he never tried to stand with me, he never offered to pay for the gas for our commute, he didn't even think twice. Deep down, I wanted to tell him to use that extra $1.50 for his bus fare to get to work.

But the truth is, I never carried much anger or resentment toward Joe after that summer. He didn't know any better. The source of my bitterness was much bigger than one person—the *source* was the *system*. As young and naïve college kids, Joe and I stepped into a system set up by hundreds of years of injustice. The disparity that caused Joe to come out on top without any extra effort was the bitter fruit of generation after generation of unfair treatment.

That's what hurt.

That was the tough pill to swallow.

That's the bitterness I refused to let go of and carried around for years.

For the past two chapters, John and I have unpacked several ways racial division has caused pain. By now, we hope you see that racial tension is less about a single isolated event and more about a culmination of millions of little ones. A single summer in a mailroom is one thing, but when enough of those events stack up on top of each other, it hurts. That pain doesn't just go away. It leaves a wound.

The question is, What do we do with our wounds?

Pain is inevitable, but does that mean we are destined to drag around baggage like an overzealous family trekking through an airport? Are we doomed to enter into every conversation about race like a ticking time bomb, triggered with one wrong word?

Or can we do something productive with our pain?

Can we heal?

Can wounds that are obstacles turn into opportunities?

I believe the answer to all those questions is a resounding yes! This chapter is about learning how to let go of all your past pain so you can move forward in the present. But if you want to heal, I mean really heal, you will have to learn the art of forgiveness. And to forgive properly, you have to be willing to run toward your pain, which is harder than it sounds, especially in a culture that expends so much energy running away from it.

Forgive or Forget?

You've probably heard the old adage *forgive and forget.*

That sounds great on paper, and I like the sentiment, but I'm not sure forgetting is the best strategy. You can't heal from centuries of pain by pretending like they never happened. Unfortunately, *forgive and forget* tends to look more like *push your feelings down and pretend they aren't there.* But that doesn't work. At least, not in the long run. The trick to healing isn't forgetting; it's the opposite. We have to remember our pain, and we have to go straight into it. Because from there, we can learn how to forgive.

Memory is crucial. Another old adage is *Those who forget the past are bound to repeat it.* Remember, this book is not about getting amnesia; it's about acknowledging what happened so we know what to forgive.

The better question is, Can you forgive even though the pain is real?

Let me come right out and say it: *For Black people, that means we have to forgive White people of previous and present injustices. And we have to do it while not harboring hatred and racism toward White people.*

That's a big ask; how do those words sit with you?

If they are a bit unsettling, that is the point. If you love holding on to your bitterness, you may be ready to close this book right about now. But before you do, let me say this: you are reading this book because you want to be a voice that fights for racial healing. But what I've noticed over the years is that nothing echoes more loudly than unforgiveness. Those who haven't forgiven aren't creating new content; they are just repeating their pain. The people who are bringing cutting-edge and helpful words to the racial conversation have all let go of a lot of their bitterness. Those who have forgiven have fresh and exciting things to say; those who have not are just repeating and harping on their bitterness, because nothing echoes more loudly than unforgiveness.

Voice or Echo?

Jesus once said, "Out of the abundance of the heart his mouth speaks" (Luke 6:45, ESV). The words that come out of our mouths are indicators of what is truly going on in us. Which means, if you want to take inventory of your internal world, pay attention to the transcript of the words you say in a given day.

The condition of the soul is always at the tip of the tongue.

For example, it's easy to tell when someone is harboring bitterness. When a person refuses to forgive, they will just say something on repeat over and over and over. It reverberates like an echo:

"I still can't believe he . . ."

"She shouldn't have . . ."

"They can't seem to . . ."

Does anyone in your life sound like a broken record? Maybe you are that person for others.

I don't look forward to hanging out with some people because I know exactly what I'm going to hear every time. It's never fresh. It's never convicting. It's never life-giving. And it's always draining.

I don't know about you, but I want to surround myself with

people who realize God is always up to something new. I want to be around people who recognize that God is always ready to speak and move us toward unity. And I want to be that person for others. They say misery loves company, which is true, but I say Kingdom-minded people love company too.

The quickest way to know exactly what you need to forgive is to pay attention to your words.

Maybe you need to forgive a person who has inflicted pain on you.

Maybe you need to forgive a system that has kept you down.

Whoever or whatever it is, God is ready to heal you.

If you want to be that person for others, it starts with letting go of the bitterness you've been storing in that back room of your *heart*. Can you give God the keys to those locked doors in your *heart*? Can you trade in your bitterness for more of God's presence? Remember, forgiving doesn't mean you have to forget; it means you are letting go of any anger, ill intent, or resentment you feel toward the person or thing that caused the pain. Whenever you are ready to let God into that place in your *heart*, he is prepared to fill that space with more of himself.

Are you a voice of truth or just an echo of pain? If you get really good at forgiveness, it will fix that echo problem real quick, because nothing echoes more loudly than unforgiveness.

"Father, Forgive Them"

In the final hours of Jesus's life, he was betrayed by one of his disciples, abandoned by the rest, arrested in a garden, put on trial and mocked in front of the high priest (and then again in front of Pilate), whipped, made to wear a crown of thorns, and forced to carry his cross—all the while being ridiculed by the people who had followed him.

Crucifixion was a terrible form of murder that combined physical pain and emotional humiliation. And the Romans perfected the art.

When Jesus finally got his cross to Golgotha, the Roman soldiers flipped him over and began driving nails into his hands. It's in that moment that Jesus uttered the most illogical sentence the world has ever heard: "Father, forgive them, for they do not know what they are doing" (Luke 23:34).

People always want to know why bad things happen to good people. But the reason I'm a Christian is because something bad happened to a perfect person. The Bible says, "God made him who had no sin to be sin for us, so that in him we might become the righteousness of God" (2 Cor. 5:21). In the greatest picture of undeserved forgiveness the world has ever seen, Jesus went to the cross so that you and I could be forgiven. And while he was experiencing that pain for us, he wasn't even holding on to resentment toward the very people inflicting the pain.

That's forgiveness.

He didn't run away from the pain; he ran through it.

He didn't avoid the humiliation; he hung in it.

He didn't hide from his wounds; he embraced them. And it's because of his wounds that we are healed (Isa. 53:5).

Forgiveness doesn't always make sense. In fact, if you can explain an act of forgiveness with logic, it probably isn't as radical as it should be. The example Jesus gave us doesn't make any sense on paper. Forgiveness, in its rawest form, surprises the distributor as it sets the offender free.

"Can I Hug Her?"

On October 2, 2019, I cried harder than I've cried in a long time.

The year before, an off-duty Dallas police officer named Amber Guyger entered the wrong home, accidentally walking into the residence of a twenty-six-year-old Black man named Botham Jean. Jean, an accountant, was sitting on his couch, eating a bowl of ice cream and relaxing after a long day. When Guyger saw him, she was scared. Thinking he was a thief, she shot and killed him. It was a tragic and unfortunate mistake that cost Jean his life.

October 2, 2019, was the final day of her trial. That day, Botham Jean's brother, Brandt (who was only eighteen at the time), addressed the court. Imagine sitting in front of the person who had robbed you of your only brother. Imagine looking that person in the eye. Imagine being on the stand while that person is on trial, getting ready to be punished for all the pain she inflicted on you.

How would you react? What would you say? How badly would you want to make a case to the judge and the jury that they should put her in prison and throw away the keys?

But he didn't talk to the jury at all. Instead, while the rest of the courtroom watched, Brandt spent his time on the stand speaking directly to Guyger. He looked her in the eyes, acknowledged how real the pain was, and then proceeded not only to forgive her but to tell her, "I love you just like anyone else. And I'm not going to say I hope you rot and die just like my brother did, but . . . I personally want the best for you."[1]

Brandt Jean didn't forget. He forgave.

That evening, I was relaxing on my couch after a long day, just like Jean had been doing before Guyger barged in and killed him. I started tearing up as I watched the video from the trial. This teenager was looking at a White police officer who had stolen his only brother's life. Most people would want her to rot in hell. Most people would tell her off and leave her stuck in a prison cell of shame. But instead, he reached down and forgave her.

And he didn't stop there. After speaking his peace, he turned to the judge and asked, "I don't know if this is possible, but can I give her a hug, please?"

That's when I lost it. Surrounded by cops, the two hugged for an entire minute, weeping, forgiving, and healing. I sat on my couch, bawling like a baby. I was watching someone say and act on a deep conviction of mine that is difficult to put into words. Guyger still had to go to prison, but that day she was set free from her own internal jail cell of guilt and shame.

If Brandt had chosen to stay bitter his whole life, no one would have blamed him. If he had decided to swing the keys to her internal prison cell of shame around his finger for the rest of his life, while she rotted away in guilt, no one would have blamed him. That's the normal human reaction. But forgiveness doesn't imprison; it posts bail. Instead, he chose the narrow path, the much more difficult one, that leads to life.

And not only did she heal from some of her guilt, but the length of her sentence was reduced. Guyger was facing life in prison, but instead, she was sentenced to only ten years. One juror said, "They were asking us to take an eye for an eye for Botham, and I feel like he isn't someone who would take an eye for an eye. He would turn the other cheek."[2]

That Sunday, I stood in front of my church and preached about that moving display of grace. Afterward, I was in the lobby meeting and greeting congregants and visitors. I struck up a conversation with a Black guy who regularly attends the church, and he mentioned how angry he was about the case.

"That White girl should have gotten more time," he said, fuming. "If it was a Black guy, they would have given him life in prison."

Even that beautiful picture of forgiveness and grace could not move his *heart*. And maybe you are in the same boat. Perhaps you've seen so many disparities in the distribution of justice that you now feel calloused. But remember, Jesus went to the cross for the very people who were putting nails through his hands. That's the power of forgiveness; it sets everyone free, even those who don't deserve it.

Swing Low, Sweet Chariot

I want to hear more of my Black brothers and sisters saying the same thing that Brandt said. I want us to learn the art of forgiveness. And not just saying it, but acting on it. It wasn't just Brandt's words. It was the fact that he hugged Guyger. Can we learn to hope for the best for those who have caused us pain?

I'm not saying we have to forget. We don't have to forget that our ancestors felt the merciless whip of a White slave owner or the unwelcoming stare of White faces as they ducked over to sip from a "coloreds only" water fountain.

I'm not saying we have to forget, but do you own any keys to prison cells of shame that you've got other people locked up in? Have you been milking your bitterness while they rot in their cell? What would it look like for you to set them free? To reach out and forgive? Because forgiveness may not always make sense, but it will always set you free.

We must continue to tell the stories and learn from our past. But we can do so while simultaneously letting go of the bitterness in our *hearts*. In a 2003 interview, Mamie Till, Emmett Till's mother, said, "I have not spent one moment hating."[3] After everything she'd been through, and the horrific injustice she'd experienced, she managed to keep moving forward. That's the power of forgiveness.

When I listen to Negro spirituals like "Hold On" and "Swing Low, Sweet Chariot," I can't help but think we've lost a bit of our edge. Our ancestors had a resilient spirit. They had their eyes set on the promised land and kept marching forward. I'm convinced their strength didn't come from running away from their pain; it came from running through it. They embraced their pain, they sang about it, and then they kept moving forward.

We've lost a bit of that spirit that could sing through the storms of life. I'm worried that instead of forgiving, we are just trying to forget. I'm worried that instead of facing our pain, we are just screaming and shouting about it. I'm worried that instead of admitting we are wounded, we are just pretending we are woke. We've traded in the bold spirit of our ancestors for the brittle spirit of outrage culture.

I'm convinced forgiveness is the antidote.

Instead of pretending to forget, we need to face the pain and forgive those who caused it. It's not about getting amnesia about the past; it's about acknowledging the pain and running straight into it, so we can learn to truly love our enemies.

I haven't managed to perfect the art of forgiveness, but I've come a long way. I've put in a lot of work to forgive people of previous and present injustices. And so, when Black pastors ask why I would "give away" my church to a White guy, I get to explain to them proudly that I'm not giving anything away. John and I are building something new together, which we can do with open hands because we have both put in the hard work to create a partnership grounded in trust. True collaboration is a luxury that healthy people who have let go of past pain and injustice get to enjoy. And I'm so glad we do.

Brandt Jean understood the power of forgiveness. He unlocked the prison cell of guilt that Amber Guyger was in and set her free. And he inspired a generation of people, including me, to keep doing the same.

Get Better, Not Bitter

I'll never forget the day I told my sister that Joe was making $1.50 more than I was. I'm not sure what I was hoping she would do. I guess I wanted her to be shocked, or to talk to my manager, or at the very least to give me some sympathy. But I didn't get any of those things. Instead, she looked at me and said, "That's what be happening with Black people," and then she walked away.

No surprise. No pity. No offense. No outrage. She'd been at the company for several years. She knew how things went, but she had managed to forgive the company without forgetting how things are. Instead of staying bitter, she got better and kept fighting. Eventually, she made a name for herself and spurred me on to do the same.

It wasn't quite as calm and compassionate as my mother's "jus' keep walkin', babee," but it was what I needed. My sister told me to double down and work harder, and that's exactly what I did. I could've stayed bitter at Joe, at the company, at an entire system, but instead, I turned the frustration into fuel and worked harder than anyone else. I may have been just a mailroom employee at some large corporation, but I resolved to be the best mailroom employee that large corporation had ever seen.

And I know some of you are thinking I shouldn't have to double down just to prove myself or that I was wasting my time. But I can assure you that doubling down and working harder is not a race issue—it's an excellence issue. As a kid, I watched an episode of *The Oprah Winfrey Show* and she said a line that got etched into my DNA: "Excellence is the best deterrent to racism."[4]

Excellence is agnostic. While it does not hinder us from experiencing bias, it is fuel that can help us *bypass* racism.

Instead of pretending like the job was beneath me, I showed up early every day, dressed fresh to death, and delivered every last piece of mail like I was bringing a classified package to the president. Every single one was on time, delivered with a smile.

I didn't forget. I forgave.

And I didn't just deliver mail; I took the time to converse with people. One person I got to know was the head of training and development. By the end of the summer, she brought me on as her right hand. And by the next summer, I was facilitating training sessions to the same employees I had delivered mail to.

That mailroom was an incubator for so much.

I thought I got promoted to the Training and Development Department, but the truth is, I started working in it the first time I applied a stamp in that mailroom to a nine-by-twelve-inch envelope (and yes, I'm still scarred from that mailroom with knowing precise envelope sizes). That mailroom WAS the Training and Development Department. And so is your job, your home, your community, your church. You're in a Training and Development Department now—learning the art of forgiveness by getting in those reps. Because forgiveness may not have a formula, but it will always set you free.

"Do Not Hold This Sin Against Them"

One of the most potent pictures of forgiveness in scripture is the story of Stephen—the New Testament's first martyr. His bio is short, but it hits home fast. He was known as a man full of faith, wisdom, and the Holy Spirit. But one day, he got in a heated debate with some people who didn't like him and ended up preaching a sermon that pushed them over the edge. The result was not good. The crowd started killing Stephen by pelting him with stones.

Before his death, scripture says he "gazed intently" toward an opened heaven where he saw Jesus standing at the right hand of God (Acts 7:55–56, NASB 1995). Which is interesting because all throughout the Bible, Jesus is referred to as *sitting* next to the Father. But here, while Stephen faced vast injustice, we see Jesus standing up for him.

Does anyone else find that incredibly comforting?

Remember, as I mentioned in Chapter 2, my first exposure to racism was a rock flying at my mother. Maybe during that time, Jesus was standing for us too. Maybe he always stands with the oppressed.

But here's something we don't ponder enough in this *everything-is-sugary-sweet* culture we are immersed in: **Jesus standing didn't stop the stones!** And you and I standing up for diversity won't always stop them either.

We might not be threatened with physical stones, but comments can pile up on a well-meaning post in our timelines that feel like stones crushing our sincerity. A cold shoulder from a family member can feel like an oncoming rock punishing us for just simply not laughing at an off-color joke. When those moments happen, we need to take a page out of Stephen's playbook and *gaze upward*. Pain is real, but when we learn to *glance* at our hurts but *gaze* toward heaven, we can begin to sound more like Jesus to an onlooking world.

When you and I are most *rejected*, heaven says we are most *received*!

And so, what does that mean for us today? Like Stephen, we need to learn the art of *glancing* at injustice but *gazing* at heaven. When Stephen does that, watch how he is able to respond to this horrible situation: "While they were stoning him, Stephen prayed, 'Lord Jesus, receive my spirit.' Then he fell on his knees and cried out, 'Lord, do not hold this sin against them'" (Acts 7:59–60).

What? That's what Stephen was thinking about during his last moments?

On paper, there is no reason for Stephen to use his final

breaths to ask God to *forgive* the very people who are murdering him, but watch what happens when he does—this is the fruit of forgiveness.

A young man named Saul was standing nearby, watching Stephen forgive the people who were killing him. At the time, Saul approved of the execution, but everything about his life was about to change. He didn't know it yet, but he was about to become the Apostle Paul, the greatest missionary in the New Testament outside of Jesus.

I believe Stephen's reaction to the stoning played a part in Paul's conversion. It seems that Stephen's prayers for God to forgive the men murdering him had a greater impact than he ever could've known. Augustine once said, "If Stephen had never prayed, Paul had never preached." Paul was not converted by seeing Stephen *rescued from that situation*; he was converted by seeing the forgiveness Stephen was willing to *extend in that situation*.

I don't think we realize just how fruitful our forgiveness will be. Stephen forgave, and the fruit of that forgiveness far exceeded his life.

It's time for us to do the same.

Time to Forgive

Now it's your turn. No matter how much pain you've experienced, can you look at the person putting a nail through your hand and say, "Father, forgive them, for they don't know what they do"?

And can you do it over and over again? Because forgiveness

doesn't have a formula. When Peter asked Jesus how many times he has to forgive, Jesus tells him, "Seventy times seven" (Matt. 18:22, KJV). That doesn't mean we have to forgive 490 times; it means there is no formula for forgiveness. You just keep forgiving and forgiving until you feel like you can't forgive anymore, then you forgive again.

Are you ready to do the same? Or are you still too angry to let go?

If your reaction is to harbor your bitterness, you are in good company. In Luke's telling of the story, the disciples felt overwhelmed by the request to forgive and cried out to Jesus, asking him to increase their faith (Luke 17:5). But Jesus knew that wasn't what they needed. He replied, "If you have faith as small as a mustard seed, you can say to this mulberry tree, 'Be uprooted and planted in the sea,' and it will obey you" (Luke 17:6).

Did you catch that?

The disciples asked for an increase of faith, but Jesus didn't grant it. Instead, he told them they needed to start exercising the faith they already had. In other words, this wasn't a *faith* issue; it was a *footstep* issue. The disciples didn't need more faith; they needed to start taking some steps to put their faith into action.

Mulberry trees were known for having deep roots—removing them was incredibly challenging. Unforgiveness works the same way. The roots run deep, and uprooting them is a process. Sometimes we need to repeat it over and over again.

So let's get practical and take some steps to uproot our unforgiveness together. Grab a journal (or just a piece of paper) and a pen. I'm serious. We are going to begin uprooting your bitterness by processing your pain. Start by answering this question:

What is the biggest source of bitterness in your life?

Think about one thing you are angry about and then take your time tracing that anger back to its source by writing out every detail you can think of about the original incident.

Who was there?

What did they say? What did they do?

Why do you think they said or did that thing?

How did it make you feel?

Take your time writing out your response to these questions. Don't worry, you don't ever have to share this with anyone if you don't want to, so don't hold back. Write out every emotion you remember feeling when you experienced the injustice.

Once you write it all out, if you are ready to take another step, talk through what you wrote with someone you trust. This could be your spouse, a good friend, or a paid professional like a counselor or therapist. Talk to that person about the incident and the bitterness you are holding on to, and watch how the bitterness begins to lose the grip it has on your *heart* every time you shine a light on it.

Revisiting the pain isn't easy, but every time we confront it, we are pulling up the mulberry tree. The roots of our unforgiveness may run deep, but if we practice processing the pain enough, our unforgiveness will eventually be "uprooted and planted in the sea."

Check Your Vitals

IMPLEMENT HEALTHY HEART
HABITS IN YOUR LIFE

JOHN SIEBELING

Since 2008, I have been making an annual trip to Dallas, Texas, to get a physical exam at the Cooper Clinic, a nonprofit founded by Kenneth Cooper, a pioneer in aerobic exercise and health. The clinic offers all-encompassing, world-class checkups for CEOs, business leaders, and individuals with high-stress jobs. It's not cheap, and it's a sacrifice to get there, but the thorough examination always leaves me feeling better equipped to lead.

But let's be honest: physicals aren't fun; they're embarrassing. First, you have to jump on a scale that reminds you about all the weight you haven't lost yet, and then you have to put on one of those revealing, backless robes and let the doctor poke and prod at your midsection (which probably isn't as hard as you'd like it to be). Nobody enjoys that process, but we do it because the long-term benefits are well worth the short-term annoyance.

The same is true for this spiritual heart checkup we've been taking you through.

Profiling.

Privilege.

Forgiveness.

We've covered a lot of ground so far. How are you doing? Are you still with us? As the stethoscope has glided across your chest, these topics may have made you press back on that crumbling tissue paper on the examination table. *Heart* work may not be easy, but I promise you, the long-term benefits are well worth the sacrifice.

But imagine if I got to the end of my physical, and the doctor said, "John, your blood work doesn't look great," and then he turned and walked out the door without giving me any practical steps forward. I'd be surprised and would probably want my money back. The goal of a physical is not just to identify problems; the goal is to establish a game plan to help you get better. What I love about the Cooper Clinic is they give you all of your results and a strategy in one day. They don't just tell you what is wrong; they set you up to take some immediate steps toward health.

That's my objective for this chapter. Before we rush off to Part Three and Part Four, where we give you lots of proactive ways to open your hands and get in the game, let's talk about some practical ways to implement healthy *heart* habits into your life that will set you up for long-term spiritual health.

Let this chapter be that probing stethoscope that not only

shows you the condition of your *heart* but guides you on the path toward health. Because as uncomfortable as it is, the old proverb reminds us, "Above all else, guard your *heart*, / for everything you do flows from it" (Prov. 4:23, emphasis added).

Crisis or Conviction?

I started going to the Cooper Clinic ten years ago because I was having heart palpitations. They can be really scary, especially when you don't know what is causing them. So I decided it was time to take a big step, and jumped on a plane to Dallas.

By the end of the checkup, the doctor had it figured out. We discovered one of the causes of my heart palpitations. Allergies can get really bad in Memphis, and at the time, I was taking allergy medicine every day. The doctor explained that I needed to slow down my intake of that medication.

Relieved that it wasn't something much worse, I got up to leave. But unfortunately, the doctor wasn't finished. He then explained that I was twenty pounds overweight and was chugging way too much coffee every day to try to make it through the stressful season of work I was in.

That part was not as easy to hear. But I knew he was right—I had to change. Fortunately, I am pretty competitive and goal-oriented. Losing weight became a game for me. I changed my diet, established a new workout routine, and was able to get down to my target weight faster than the doctor expected.

Crisis averted.

But here's the embarrassing part. Once I hit my target weight, I let my guard down. It started small, but one extra hamburger turned into two; two shakes while I was on the road traveling turned into three; and before I knew it, I was back to living the same lifestyle I was before the physical.

You know exactly where this story is heading, don't you?

Unfortunately, I ended right back at the same weight I was at before my trip to Dallas. That was a challenging moment. I specifically remember leaving Shake Shack one night feeling a deep conviction from the Holy Spirit that something needed to change. I didn't just need to lose the weight; I needed to become a healthy person.

If I wanted a healthy *heart*, I needed some healthy habits.

And so I stopped looking for a quick fix and started implementing some healthy habits that allowed me to not just lose the weight, but keep it off.

The first time I lost weight, I was responding to a *crisis*, but the second time, I was responding to a deep *conviction* that it was time to change. There is a big difference between those two things. The former is a short-term fix; the latter leads to long-term freedom. There is a time and a place to react to a crisis, but the real goal is to be transformed by a deep *heart* conviction.

The same principle applies to the conversation about race.

Oftentimes, we try to right racial wrongs, to avoid criticism, or to react to a crisis. But a healthy heart responds from a deep conviction that racism is wrong.

Of course, there is nothing wrong with reacting to a crisis. George Floyd's death was a tragedy, and in the months that followed, the protests shed a ton of light on issues that had been in the dark for too long. Reacting to a crisis is important, but we are writing this book because we need a deep, *heart* conviction that racial unity is needed.

When enough people have that conviction, we won't need to wait for another crisis before we see change happening. We want to encourage you to be a person who is in the fight for racial equity every day. That way, we will be ready when the storms hit, but we will also continue making progress in times of peace.

Like my journey toward not only losing weight, but keeping it off, we need to develop some healthy *heart* habits so that we will become the type of people who fight for racial justice for the right reasons. So let's build some healthy *heart* habits.

Healthy Heart Habit #1: Stay Humble

During his ministry, Jesus was always telling parables designed to be *heart* checks. One day, while talking to "certain people who were convinced of their own righteousness, and who despised all others" (Luke 18:9, WEB), he told them a parable about two characters, a Pharisee and a tax collector. A tax collector was like a modern-day IRS worker. Except they were even less popular in those days because they were Jewish people who had sold out and worked for "the man"—the Roman government—and extorted other Jews on taxes for their personal gain.

Although the passage from Luke doesn't deal directly with race, it teaches a valuable lesson about the danger of discrimination when we start thinking we are better than a certain people group. "Two men went up to the temple to pray, one a Pharisee and the other a tax collector. The Pharisee stood by himself and prayed: 'God, I thank you that I am not like other people—robbers, evildoers, adulterers—or even like this tax collector. I fast twice a week and give a tenth of all I get'" (Luke 18:10–12).

I love how even though the Pharisee was praying by himself, he felt the need to justify his behavior, listing all the things that made him better than others. He wasn't an extortionist, wasn't unjust, didn't cheat on his wife, and he certainly wasn't like that tax collector on the other side of the temple.

Pause for a moment, particularly if you are White. Have you ever done this comparison thing when it comes to the issue of race? Do you ever catch yourself saying things like, "I am a good person. I'm not like my ancestors. I actually love everybody. I mean, I went on a mission trip once. I'm not like those White supremacists who marched in Charlottesville! I'm not like that politician who wore blackface!"

But remember who Jesus was speaking to here. His audience was "certain people who were convinced of their own righteousness." Just because you don't fall into those extreme categories doesn't mean you haven't nursed a negative bias about certain people. If you find yourself constantly convincing yourself that you aren't as bad as someone else, that's a sign it's time to take inventory of your *heart*.

Meanwhile, on the other side of the temple, the tax collector prayed a different kind of prayer:

> But the tax collector stood at a distance. He would not even look up to heaven, but beat his breast and said, "God, have mercy on me, a sinner."
>
> I tell you that this man, rather than the other, went home justified before God. For all those who exalt themselves will be humbled, and those who humble themselves will be exalted.
>
> (LUKE 18:13–14)

The two men could not be more different. The Pharisee was trying to be the justifier; the tax collector knew he needed a justifier. The Pharisee was proud. The tax collector was humble. And Jesus is crystal clear that the latter is the way forward; humility is a healthy *heart* habit that leads to long-term health and sustainability. God isn't searching for men and women who have it all together. He is looking for people who know they need a savior.

Because humility is fertile ground for reconciliation.

And this isn't the only story in scripture about the power that comes from this healthy *heart* habit. Humility is a central theme all throughout the Bible.

Something like Scales

The Apostle Paul is a hero of the Christian faith. He took the gospel farther than anyone before him, planting at least fourteen churches and writing almost half the books in the New Testament along the way.

If anyone had the right to brag, it was Paul. And yet in his letter to his protégé Timothy, he wrote, "Here is a trustworthy saying that deserves full acceptance: Christ Jesus came into the world to save sinners—of whom *I am the worst*" (1 Tim. 1:15, emphasis added).

Paul, the man who had every right to gloat about his impressive accomplishments, referred to himself as the worst of sinners. Why? Because Paul understood that humility is a habit of a healthy *heart*.

So how do we stay humble? No matter how high he rose, Paul's strategy was that he never forgot how low he had been. Remember, before he was Paul, his name was Saul, and he was wreaking havoc on the church. He was a Jewish Pharisee who adamantly opposed the spread of Christianity and did everything he could to stomp out the movement, including murder.

Paul hated people who didn't think the same way as he did.

But one day, while he was walking down the road to Damascus, to arrest some more Christians, God intervened. A bright light shone all around Saul, knocking him to the ground and blinding him for three days. But when a man named Ananias prayed for him, the Bible says, "something like scales fell from Saul's eyes, and he could see again" (Acts 9:18).

Once the scales fell off, Paul stopped killing and started saving.

Once the scales fell off, Paul traded in his old mindset for a new one.

Once the scales fell off, the persecutor became a prophet.

Paul was able to admit that he was wrong. And when he did, everything about his life started changing. He stopped putting up walls between the people who didn't think like him, and he started tearing down walls in the church. Paul paved the way for the gospel to spread not only to the Jews but also to the gentiles. He is one of the primary reasons Christianity spread to the ends of the earth. And it all began because he was humble enough to admit that he was wrong.

Approaching conversations about *privilege* with an open mind takes humility.

Approaching conversations about *profiling* with an open *heart* takes humility.

And approaching conversations about *forgiveness* with open hands takes an awful lot of humility.

Humility leads to open hands. If we want to be agents of reconciliation, we need to get in the habit of practicing humility.

How to Stay Humble

Staying humble sounds good on paper, but how do we do it? Jesus gives us a great answer to that question. One day when his disciples asked him how to pray, he gave them a model we call the Lord's Prayer. Listen to one of the lines from the famous prayer: "Your kingdom come, your will be done, on earth as it is in heaven" (Matt. 6:10).

We love asking God for *our will* to be done, but how often do we ask God for *his will* to be done? If you had a transcript of your prayers from the past month, what percentage would be about you asking for things you wanted? And what percentage would be about you surrendering and trying to realign your *heart* with God's?

Here's your practical step to staying humble: *pray the Lord's Prayer every morning.* I've done this for several years now, and it has transformed my life.

Things may not always work out the way you want them to, but when you are in a real trust relationship with God, you learn to start seeing that it is actually God's plan unfolding when plans change.

Are you humble enough to trust that God knows what he is doing? If so, *disappointments* are opportunities to get *reappointed* with God. I know that's easier said than done, but practice makes perfect.

Humble *hearts* say not "my will," but "your will" be done.

Humble *hearts* trade in White knuckles for white flags.

Are you willing to lay your old mentalities at the foot of the cross? Are you willing to admit that some of your beliefs about people who don't look like you may be wrong?

Humble *hearts* lead to open hands, so try praying the Lord's Prayer every morning to practice *staying humble*.

Healthy Habit #2: Stay Hungry

Dwayne "The Rock" Johnson is a different type of specimen. He is so strong that his muscles have muscles. And he has to look that way because while the stunts his characters pull off in movies are the farthest things from realistic, they are way more believable because of the way he looks.

Recently, I listened to an interview where he was asked how he keeps up his physique. His answer stunned me. His workouts are one thing, but his diet is ridiculous. He eats more than five thousand calories every single day, just to maintain what he already has.

That's a lot of pasta.

And if I'm honest, that actually sounds like it would be fun for a few days. But imagine living with that burden every day. Sure, he can take one day off here and there, but if he ate like a regular person for a month or two, he wouldn't be The Rock anymore. It's not just hard work to get there; it's incredibly challenging to maintain.

The Rock has to stay hungry.

Last year, Wayne and I were in the pool one evening, relaxing after a workout. We started talking about race and the church, and I told him how much pressure I feel to stay up-to-date with all of the issues surrounding the conversation. He encouraged me, telling me how far along I am in my journey, but I still couldn't shake the feeling. The truth is, twenty years into engaging in conversations about race and doing my best to stay aware, I feel like I have more questions than ever before.

The race conversation is evolving every day, and I feel a healthy pressure to keep up with it in real time. What I was trying to say to Wayne that day is that even though I've put in a lot of work, I feel a healthy burden to continue learning. I need to stay hungry and continue consuming five thousand calories of information, relational experience, and empathy toward racial challenges every day.

What about you? Are you still hungry? At your core, do you feel a burden to continue learning everything you can about the race conversation?

I know it's not easy, but you have to stay with it because this isn't a problem to solve; it's a tension to be managed.

When Wayne and I first launched a three-week series called "Black Fists, White Knuckles," we quickly realized it needed to be an ongoing conversation. We've kept at it by writing this book, delivering more sermons, and dedicating a segment of our podcast, *Leadership in Black and White*, to include a thought about race every month. The journey never ends.

Unfortunately, the crisis management model held by many churches and organizations treats race issues like fires to put out. What if, instead, we stay hungry, get ahead of the game, and find opportunities to have conversations that prevent us from having fires in the first place?

The word *relevant* gets tossed around a lot these days, but it really just means being able to talk about the things going on at the moment in the culture around us. The Apostle Paul was relevant. He had his finger on the pulse of his culture and was able to speak the language of his day to preach the gospel.

I don't know about you, but I want to be able to do the same. These days that means we need to stay hungry. We need to continue consuming information about what is currently happening in the world.

Don't let this healthy habit overwhelm you; just take it one day at a time. Devote ten to fifteen minutes each day to learning one new thing about the race conversation. You can do this on your commute to work or school by finding a podcast that you enjoy. If you don't already have one, start with *Leadership in Black and White*. Not only is it a great starting point, but during the episodes, Wayne and I are always bringing up new resources to help you stay up-to-date.

I've been having conversations about race for several decades, but I still learned a lot in 2020. That year reminded me how far I still have to go, because the more you learn, the more you realize how much you don't know. The day you stop learning is the day you begin your decline toward being irrelevant. Keep pressing in and keep learning.

Healthy *hearts* never stop learning and growing, so stay hungry.

Track Your Progress

I have an Apple Watch that I use exclusively for working out. When I jump on the treadmill or my Peloton, I throw it on because it tracks my stats for me. I love examining the data and tracking my progress. That's what keeps me going back to the treadmill, especially on the days when I'm just not feeling it.

You may find that implementing this strategy for the information you are consuming inspires you to stay with it. You don't need an Apple Watch to do this; just start a spreadsheet and begin keeping track of all the books you've read and podcasts you've listened to about racial unity. That way, you can set monthly and yearly goals for yourself, monitor your progress along the way, and know whether you are hitting those goals. This strategy also gives you a place to write down quotations that affected you from your reading so you can revisit them from time to time.

I love looking back at my Apple Watch, especially when I crushed the goals I set up for myself. It inspires me to *stay hungry* and push myself even more the next day. If you are an analytical person like me, try keeping track of the amount of content you are consuming on the race conversation so you can celebrate the progress you are making over time.

Healthy Habit #3: Stay Hopeful

Recently, a White friend of mine told me about a series of conversations he had with his father after George Floyd's murder. His father is as type A as it comes. He's spent his entire adult life either in the army or in civil service. He has a strong personality and even stronger convictions. When he believes something is right, there is no convincing him otherwise.

His father started talking about how tired he was of all the riots and protests, and how he believed the officer who put his knee on Floyd's neck was following his training. That wasn't surprising to my friend. He'd heard his father say similar things his entire life.

My friend could've lost hope years ago that his father would ever change. He could've decided to throw in the towel and take the path of least resistance. But my friend understands that a healthy *heart* stays hopeful.

So he pushed back against his father's opinion. The two argued for a while until my friend asked, "Have you watched the footage?"

"I have not."

"I have," he said, "and I read the transcripts. We aren't saying Floyd was innocent. We are saying he never even had a chance to go to court or serve time in prison. Instead, they killed him in the street while he begged for his life. This isn't as clear-cut as you are trying to make it."

He went on to explain the abuse of power and how he believes things need to change. As you can imagine, the conversation wasn't open to much debate. Eventually, both men grew tired of going in circles and changed the subject.

People are predictable, and when you get the same response from someone every time you talk to them, it can be tough to hold on to the hope that they will ever change.

But healthy hearts stay hopeful.

It's easy to fall into the mindset that some of our friends and loved ones will never change their minds, but healthy *hearts* don't listen to that lie.

Think about how many people probably wrote Paul off back in the day when he was persecuting the church. As they ran for their lives, they probably weren't thinking, *I bet that guy will be a church planter one day.*

Can we stop and acknowledge something real quick? If God is strong enough to take the scales off Paul's eyes, he's strong enough to do the same for anyone. If someone in your life seems to be so deeply entrenched in their racist ways that you've stopped praying or reaching out, it's time to change the way you think. We need to get our hope back. No one is too far gone.

Three weeks later, my friend's father approached him, unprompted. He sat him down and said, "I've thought a lot about what you said, and then I watched the footage. I was wrong. We have a system set in place, and they didn't use it. That wasn't right, and neither was I."

That's it. It was as diplomatic as you would expect, and that may sound small to you, but it was a massive victory. It takes a lot of humility for someone to utter such words. Humility is a progression, and that was a huge first step. And any time people show any signs of humility, it should give us hope.

Think back again to Paul's journey toward humility. It wasn't immediate; it was incremental. You can see this even in the way he described himself, from "the least of the apostles" (1 Cor. 15:9), to "the least of all the Lord's people" (Eph. 3:8), all the way to the "worst" of sinners (1 Tim. 1:15).

What was going on here? Did Paul struggle with low self-esteem, or was he going through the progression of a person coming to grips with how harmful his original bias was? Humility is a process, so anytime you see it happening, get your hopes up!

I'm so thankful conversations like the one my friend had with his father are happening all over our country and all over the world. Let that fill your *heart* with hope. Scales are falling off, and we are finally beginning to see each other eye to eye. And although it may not be happening quite as quickly or drastically as we want it to, the important thing is that it is happening. We are moving in the right direction.

In the church, we are great at celebrating the 180-degree types of turns. Those types of moments get video testimonies and stage time on Sundays. But I think it's time we start celebrating the 8-degree turns as well. When we begin stringing enough little wins together, we will eventually look back and won't believe how far we've come.

One practical way to stay hopeful is to constantly remind ourselves about the end of the story. Even in the tough moments, there is hope, because no matter how dark the night may be, we know that God wins in the end. C. S. Lewis once famously said, "If you read history you will find that the Christians who did most for the present world were precisely those who thought most of the next."[1] Healthy habits create healthy *hearts*, so get in the habit of spending a couple of minutes every day reflecting on the truth that in the end, every tribe, tongue, and nation will be worshiping together (Rev. 7:9). That way you can become the type of person who can proclaim that hope to the world!

Press On

Imagine the first morning that Paul woke up and got ready to help build the church. How awkward was that first day? He was joining arms with the people whom he not only hated but who also hated him. Remember, he threw some of their friends in prison and had others killed. We love to celebrate Paul's conversion story, but think about the baggage he had to work through afterward.

God forgave him immediately, but let's be honest: people aren't always as quick to do the same. It turns out, humility is not the only thing that works in chronological order—relationship repair does too. Can you imagine the stares he got?

We all have pain in our past. We may not have been killing people and throwing them in prison for thinking differently than us, but we've all said and done some things we wish we could take back. Maybe you grew up hearing the N-word thrown around casually so often that it wove itself into your subliminal mindset. Or perhaps you grew up describing a White person in a derogatory way and still find yourself referring to that description when you feel wronged.

If we aren't careful, that shame can make us feel unqualified to be a part of reconciliation. But that's a lie. Remember the *heart* posture of the tax collector. There is power in confessing our need for a savior, and there is room in this fight for every *heart* that is ready to become humble, hungry, and hopeful.

One of my favorite parts about Paul is that he kept going. He didn't let the pain in his past hold him back from the promises ahead of him. In his letter to the church in Philippi, he wrote, "But one thing I do: Forgetting what is behind and straining toward what is ahead, I *press on* toward the goal to win the prize for which God has called me heavenward in Christ Jesus" (Phil. 3:13–14, emphasis added). Sometimes I wonder if Paul was writing that more for himself than anyone else.

We need to learn to preach that message to ourselves over and over again.

There may be pain in our past, but there is promise in our future. When I see everything that is happening today, I am incredibly hopeful. We are making progress. It may be two steps forward and one step back and then one to the side, but together we are moving forward. Don't give up. We have to face forward and keep pressing on toward the promises ahead.

After I had that first physical in Dallas, it still took me a couple of sobering moments to realize that in order to protect my *heart*, I needed to change the habits of my *heart*. But once I did, I began a journey toward true transformation. No matter what Part Two has revealed about the current state of your *heart*, there is hope. Start some new and healthy habits, and watch how your *heart* begins to transform.

Healthy habits create healthy *hearts*, and healthy hearts lead to open hands.

Stay humble.

Stay hungry.

And stay hopeful.

TRAVEL LIGHT

Congratulations on making it this far. Take a few more moments to think through everything you've learned. What did God reveal to you when you asked him to search your *heart*?

We have a long journey toward racial healing ahead of us, and the trip will not be easy. However, it will be way more enjoyable if we aren't traveling with so much baggage, so before you go any farther, take a second to start building some healthy *heart* habits by taking these two action steps:

Forgive someone: Remember what Wayne said: forgiveness doesn't always make sense, but it will always set you free. If you are holding on to some resentment, it is weighing you down. Take a minute and write a letter to someone you need to forgive. Don't worry, you don't need to send it to them; it's just cathartic to write it out. This may be someone you know personally, or it may be a public figure who hurt you from a distance. Either way, holding on to the bitterness isn't going to help you move forward.

Apologize to someone: Maybe you've caused pain for someone else. If so, take some time to humble yourself by reaching out and asking that person for forgiveness. Even if you feel like they have a part to play, own your piece. Don't worry about how your apology will be received. Your job is simply to say "I'm sorry" and let it go. You'll be amazed at how far the word *sorry* will go.

PART THREE

Household

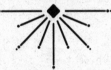

We are living in a historical moment.

Years from now, when our great-great-grandchildren read about this moment in their history books, what will they learn? Will they read only about pain and polarization? Or will they read about people who put aside their differences and came together?

The *heart* work you did in Part Two was to prepare you for the rest of this book. Now that you've looked inward, you are ready to shift your focus outward. It's time to talk about your *household*.

Ultimately, we are heading toward talking about how to create churches that look like heaven. But sometimes, we fall into the trap of sitting in the grandstands and throwing stones at our churches so that we don't have to take an honest look at our own home. The truth is, the first step for creating diverse churches is inviting that same diversity into our homes. What type of home will our children and their children inherit?

What if it's a household where open-handed conversations about God and race are the norm?

What if it's a household where unity is the rule and racism is rare?

What if it's a household where racial healing is the reality instead of a far-off dream?

All of that is possible. But we are the ones responsible for getting us there. We are building the *households* that future generations will live in, and that makes us history makers! You are here for a reason. The Bible says, "From one man he made all the nations, that they should inhabit the whole earth; and he marked out their appointed times in history and the boundaries of their lands" (Acts 17:26). From the beginning, God had a plan for your life. It's no accident that you live in the time and place you live in; you are here for such a time as this!

Influencing history begins with influencing your *household*. We all come from different homes, and the home you grew up in shaped you. And whether it shaped you in a positive or negative way, you now have a home to shape, so we will show you how to fight for diversity in your home. After that, we'll discuss your friends. Does everyone in your social circle look like you? If so, it's time to meet some new people. From there, we'll talk about how to use your influence to help bring reconciliation as you go throughout your day and interact with others through social media.

Get ready, because we aren't going to hold back; we want to equip you with some of the tangible steps you need. The home you are building, the social circle you have, and the things you post online all matter. It's time to get practical and learn how to have open-handed conversations about race. Remember, we are in this together. As the writer of Hebrews says, "we are surrounded by such a great cloud of witnesses" (Heb. 12:1). History is calling you forward, and those who came before you are cheering you on.

You have a part to play in this story.

Are you ready to be a part of the solution in your community?

Are you ready to help the church you attend move forward?

The next step is to build a *household* that looks like heaven!

Have an Open House

Homogeneity: *the quality or state of being all the same.*

If a species is diverse, and connected to other species, it can prosper; if the species is homogeneous, it is vulnerable.

—RICHARD KOCH

WAYNE FRANCIS

Fifty years ago, my parents migrated from Jamaica to the Bronx in pursuit of the American Dream. In those days, there was a popular sitcom called *The Jeffersons* about a Black family who moved to New York City. You've probably heard the now-famous theme song sung by Ja'Net DuBois from the opening credits:

Well we're movin' on up
To the East Side
To a deluxe apartment in the sky.

Movin' on up
To the East Side
We finally got a piece of the pie.

Those words encapsulated my dad's vision. At the time, my parents' slice of the world's infamous concrete jungle was an eight-hundred-square-foot apartment, but he worked multiple jobs to get his piece of the pie and pound a permanent stake in the place where he proudly became a citizen. After saving and searching for years, he finally found a home in the Northeast Bronx.

We were moving on up from the ghetto to the good life.

My dad was proud. But my mom was nervous.

"Are you sure?" she asked him. "Is it wise to move into that neighborhood with all those White people?"

Looking back, I think my father was doing this on purpose. He knew the risk that came with diversity, but he also knew that the benefits were worth the risk. Even though this new community would present new challenges, staying where we were, surrounded by people who looked like us, would keep us stuck, because the home can't be homogeneous.

The houses in the new neighborhood were pressed next to each other, separated only by a wall. And our backyards were conjoined like twins that could never be separated surgically. Each house had a one-car garage with a short driveway and reminded me of the row homes you see in a place like George-town, just way less bourgeois (or *boujee* as young people say).

I'll never forget riding my bike around that street. I'd zoom past the nuns who lived a few houses down, and they'd always greet me with a modest wave that looked like they were offering me communion elements.

Then I'd ride past Mr. Koch, the Orthodox Jewish man who lived next door. He was a bald White guy, and to this day, I still don't know how he kept his yarmulke on his head. I often played with his son Matthew in our front yard, and Mr. Koch would come out and have friendly conversations with me before hauling Matthew off to the synagogue down the road.

Then there were Rosie and Sam, our larger-than-life Italian neighbors who lived on the other side of us and always filled the air with the delicious aroma of penne and fresh tomato sauce. Rosie was a mean lady. She'd scream at us when our whiffle balls found her driveway, but Sam would give her a hard time for her old-world Italian tone. Then he'd give us a reassuring smile as he sat on his porch in his white tank top.

Meanwhile, tunes by Gloria Gaynor and Bob Marley wafted from our house, along with the savory scents of curry, jerk seasonings, island fruit punch, and other Jamaican fare.

We were a diverse little community. White people were no longer a group of people who lived in distant cities—they were our neighbors. And as strange as that must have been for my parents and sisters, it was all I knew. I grew up with rose (or Rosie)–colored glasses, and I loved it.

White Flight

But the Bronx began changing quickly. In 1950, more than 90 percent of the borough was White, but by 1980, that number was down to less than 33 percent.[1] Sociologists call this phenomenon *White flight*. And although our little community seemed to be immune to it for a while, all that changed when

Rosie died. I still remember Sam's children coming over to move him out of the neighborhood. Mr. Koch and Matthew left soon after and headed north to Westchester, followed by the nuns. As this happened, Black people started moving in, many of whom were Jamaicans.

Our Bronx neighborhood was becoming a mini Montego Bay (minus the mango trees and beautiful beaches). Even as a young kid, I was smart enough to recognize the pattern. Before I knew it, our diverse neighborhood became very homogeneous.

Unfortunately, this was also around the time crack cocaine became readily available. The crack epidemic hit our neighborhood hard, and addiction rates went through the roof. Demand for crack went up, and whenever there is demand, there will be supply. Gangs moved in to sell drugs, and violence skyrocketed. Times were changing fast.

For my freshman and sophomore years of high school, I attended a school in the South Bronx. I excelled in classes and even started a successful business, seeded by my favorite teacher. However, outside of the classroom, I was attracted to street culture.

I had four sisters and a very distant relationship with my dad, so running around on the periphery of gangs was fun for me. Honestly, I was too afraid of my dad to get tethered to the inner workings of street life, but that didn't stop me from picking up some bad habits. I couldn't help it.

There's a truth to that, isn't there? Given enough time, the habits of the dominant culture will eventually win. Even when we try to resist, homogeneity wears us down.

I was getting myself into quite a bit of trouble, and my dad was getting worried. One night, I came in late after a night of drinking and a run-in with a rival crew, and in his thick Jamaican accent, my dad said, "Either the streets are going to kill you, or I am."

He knew he had to do something.

Magnotta's Pizzeria

To this day, my father is the hardest working man I've ever known. He never called in sick and always had several side hustles, including opening a grocery store and bar in our neighborhood. One of his favorite sayings is "Gimme di ovah-time."

At the time, his job was up in White Plains, a city in Westchester County, about thirty miles north of the Bronx. There was a pizza parlor near his work called Magnotta's Restaurant and Pizzeria. Best pizza in New York. Every evening, after he finished his shift, he would stop in and grab a slice before heading home.

The owner was a man named Angelo Magnotta, who was every bit as Italian as his name. Picture the stereotypical caricature of an Italian New Yorker, and you are probably close. He had big beautiful blue eyes with slicked-back wet black hair, always coifed perfectly. Plus, a chest full of hair that was a velvety backdrop for the gold chain and crucifix that dangled just above his midsection. Ever since he opened his doors in 1972, he'd been committed to creating a great atmosphere and delicious pizza and ran that same restaurant for forty-seven years before finally retiring in 2019.

Over the years, my father struck up a great friendship with Angelo. One day, he was telling him how worried he was about the school I was attending.

"There's a great high school up here," Angelo said, genuinely trying to help. "Why don't you send him there?"

It was a great thought, but my father went on to explain how zoning works. "You have to send your kid to the school that matches up with your address," he told Angelo.

"Well then use my address," Angelo said without skipping a beat.

My dad thought Angelo had lost his mind. Why would a White man living in White Plains offer to do something illegal to allow his son to have a better life?

He knew there had to be a catch—a kickback.

But there wasn't.

Angelo didn't have anything to gain from the offer—it's not like we could afford to pay him—and he had a whole lot to lose. But without hesitation, he threw the offer down on the table and changed the trajectory of my life.

The Burbs

Before I knew it, I was movin' on up to the Burbs, going to school with kids who didn't look anything like me. In the Bronx we took the bus everywhere; in the Burbs the kids drove their parents' 3-Series BMWs. In the Bronx we'd cut class to pick up a ham and cheese hero from the local bodega that smelled like sun-dried urine; in the Burbs the kids were too busy crying over the 94 percent they got on their exam to cut class. In the Bronx our school was surrounded by crowded, noisy streets; in the Burbs our school was surrounded by botanic garden–level trees. Kids would bring blankets and study on the lawn between classes.

It was an entirely new world, and it was the furthest thing from homogeneous, but I loved it. And I thrived.

These two opportunities helped me see the impact of being around people of different skin hues at a very early age. Throughout my life, I've seen White and Black people working together. Looking back, Angelo took a giant risk. My father did too. Their friendship is a perfect picture of the mutual benefit of diversity that has been modeled for me repeatedly. And I'm so thankful for it. Because although fighting for diversity is a lot of work, it's worth every last bit of it.

Sometimes the best way to break down walls is to invite people to walk through the door.

Get Up, Peter

The struggle to avoid homogeneity is nothing new. For thousands of years, God has been inviting human beings to open their doors to people who don't look like them. But in the Bible, this was often a point of contention.

The Jewish people had extensive purity laws. According to these laws, gentiles were unclean. But Jesus came to offer salvation to everyone. Both Jew and gentile. And he gave his disciples a commission to take this message to ALL nations.

However, old habits die hard, so although the church was reaching out to Jews, they were still struggling to believe the gospel was also for the gentiles. They were staying homogeneous.

In Acts 10, Peter, a pillar of the early church, was traveling around, preaching the gospel. Even though he had witnessed Jesus's model for ministry firsthand, and saw his rabbi include everyone (especially those pushed to the margins), he was still struggling to preach to the gentiles.

One day he was staying with a man named Simon the tanner. A tanner is someone who turns animal skin into leather. Now, I like me some leather shoes and a motorcycle jacket, but I have no desire whatsoever to be in the shop of a taxidermist! It's a messy (and smelly) job, usually reserved for the lowest of the low. Simon probably lived on the outskirts of town. By the way, Jewish purity laws forbade anyone to work with dead animals, so Simon was both spiritually and physically unclean. And yet, the Bible tells us Peter stayed with him for some time.

Around noon, Peter was praying on Simon's roof. While lunch was in the oven, he got hungry and fell into a trance. A sheet came down from heaven, "by its four corners" (Acts 10:11), filled with all kinds of animals, and a voice said, "Get up, Peter. Kill and eat" (Acts 10:13). But he wouldn't do it, because the animals were unclean.

Isn't it interesting how we can often overlook some taboos and yet struggle with others?

Notice Peter's selective outrage. He was staying with Simon the tanner, but he was still calling certain animals unclean. And he was saying no to God in the process. I love the Bible's honesty. How can someone who is being used by God in such powerful ways still hold on to his old mindset? Peter was starting to understand the importance of including a tanner but still couldn't wrap his mind around the whole gentile thing.

The voice tried a second time, and then a third before the

sheet was taken back into heaven, leaving Peter to ponder what that was all about.

I love the detail about the sheet coming from and being taken back to heaven. It was filled with things Peter's Jewish mind would not expect to be coming from a celestial place. Could it be that the things (or people) we think are unclean and common will end up being our neighbors?

Started in a Home, but Now We're Here

This short story has massive implications. From there, Peter is invited into the home of a gentile and eventually figures out that he "should not call anyone impure or unclean" (Acts 10:28).

Think about that for a moment. Peter had a pattern of labeling people who weren't like him in derogatory ways. Many of us probably have done the same thing.

Have your misconceptions kept you from entering into certain homes?

Have your misconceptions kept you from opening your door to others?

Peter enters the house, preaches the gospel, the Holy Spirit falls, and everyone gets baptized. It's an amazing story of the first gentile converts. The events in that home opened the door for the gospel to spread to the ends of the earth.

Keeping gentiles out of the church may have been more comfortable, but it wasn't congruent with God's design for the world. Once Peter and the rest of the church finally saw this, the gospel spread quickly. Today there are some 2.3 billion

Christians worldwide, spreading across almost every nation, language, and ethnicity.[2] And it all started in one single home.

I wonder if Peter and the gentiles present in that story ever got together in heaven, remembered the walls that fell that day, and marveled at the effect it had on the entire world. I'm not sure if Drake parodies are popular in heaven, but if I were with them, you better believe I'd be singing, "*Started in a home, but now we're here.*"

So what about your home? God is always laying a sheet out in front of us, inviting us to get up and kill any prejudice holding us back from loving everyone. Could it be that God is calling you to fight against homogeneity in your own home? Could it be that God strategically placed neighbors around us who don't look like us because we are supposed to open our doors up to them and learn from them? Could the example we show our kids and our conversations with them train up world-changers who fight for all people? You have way more influence than you think. Your kids are watching. Your spouse is watching. Your friends are watching.

What if, years from now, when you are looking back on the impact you've had in helping people have open-handed conversations about *God and race*, you too get to sing, "*Started in a home, but now we're here*"?

My father gave me a gift. He taught me how to continually fight for diversity in my home. And now, it's second nature to me.

My wife, Classy, and I have raised our daughters in a home that welcomes all people. We have White friends they still call "aunt" and "uncle" to this day. Sometimes the best way to break down walls is to invite people to walk through the door.

So how do we move forward?

My father modeled four key ways to fight for diversity in the home: confidence, calmness, collaboration, and consistency. Let's look at each of these words.

Confidence

The first key to building diversity in your home is *confidence*.

My father is as Jamaican as the day is long. And one of my favorite parts about him is he has the confidence to be that way with every person he meets. It doesn't matter if he is talking to his best friend or the president; he knows who he is, and he doesn't change based on who is in the room.

People don't always know what to do with my dad at first. I've seen him walk right up to an unsuspecting new guy at church and give him a big hug while saying, "My brother from a Whiter mother," at the top of his lungs. It's a lot for some people, but by the end of the day, he always wins them over. People respect my father because he isn't trying to be someone he's not.

To be clear: I'm not telling you to do that. I'm telling you to have enough confidence to be who you are! That's what it is going to take to bring diversity into our homes.

Many Black people feel the pressure to code-switch, that is, to change our behavior based on our surroundings. I've certainly felt it. As a preacher, I've felt the urge to step up my vocabulary and act a certain way when I'm around White people.

Just fit in.

Play the part.

It's human nature. At times it feels so much simpler to be like everyone else. But that's a lie. You are uniquely wired; God knit you together in your mother's womb (Ps. 139:13). Your job is not to fit a certain mold the world is telling you to fit; your job is to have the confidence to be the person God created you to be!

One of the lines I tell my girls is, don't mute your Blackness. I want them to have confidence in who God created them to be. I want them to be proud of who they are and where they came from. The truth is, my daughters are children of the King, coheirs with Christ, created in the image of God. I want them to be a full expression of that image. They love Jamaican food, aren't afraid to ask for hot sauce, and don't feel like they need to dress or comb their hair a certain way.

People appreciate authenticity. My father may be a loud, outspoken Jamaican man, but he is the same loud, outspoken Jamaican man with every single person he comes into contact with. He never tones it down, and people learn to love him for it.

We all have an edge to us; are we willing to let the world see it? Have the confidence to be who you are.

Calmness

The second key to fighting for diversity in the home is *calmness*. The language I've been using for my daughters is I want them to be pillars, not pillows. The psalmist writes,

Then our sons in their youth
  will be like well-nurtured plants,
and our daughters will be like pillars
  carved to adorn a palace. (Ps. 144:12)

I love that imagery. People lay their heads on pillows, but they lay foundations on pillars, so I want my daughters to be pillars carved to adorn a palace.

Pillars need to be principled, but they also need to be polite. One of the first things people usually say after interacting with my girls is how respectful they are. We raised them like that on purpose. They know they have to walk a lot of different lines because of the color of their skin, so we've taught them how to deescalate things quickly. As the proverb says, "A soft answer turns away wrath, / but a harsh word stirs up anger" (Prov. 15:1, ESV). My daughters know the art of deescalating situations.

The reality is, racism is real. Some people will look down on my daughters because of the color of their skin. Until we can get justice, we need deescalation. So we teach our kids how to be confident, but we also show them how to stay calm, because confidence and calmness are not at odds with each other. We can deescalate without losing our dignity.

The Intersection of Confidence and Calmness

Jesus is the ultimate picture of confidence and calmness. When you read the Gospels, it's clear Jesus was always a step ahead of everyone, and confident that his next step was the right one. And yet, when he was persecuted, he kept his peace. When

Pilate questioned him, he stayed quiet. And while being publicly crucified, he prayed for those who were punishing him.

He mastered the art of being both confident and calm, and the result was that everyone felt welcomed around him, and he built a team that was far from homogeneous. Jesus wasn't a pillow; he was, and is, a pillar. He is the pillar—the foundation of the entire church.

Collaboration

My junior and senior years at White Plains High School were amazing. The only part I didn't enjoy was the commute. It took me about ninety minutes to get to and from school because of all the stops along the bus route. By the end of a long day of classes, the last thing I wanted to do was make the journey home. But the thing that always made the rides easier was that I knew Angelo would have a hot slice of pizza waiting for me after school. I stopped in often to say hello and grab a slice before I jumped on the bus. He never charged me either. I don't know why he was so good to us, but I've never forgotten it.

Angelo is a picture of the power of *collaboration*. The home is an intimate place, but he let us into his—literally and figuratively—and it changed my life. Sometimes the best way to break down walls is to invite people to walk through the door.

These days, when times get tough, we may be tempted to treat our home like a castle. We retreat, dig a moat, and pull up the drawbridge so that we can be the king or queen of our space.

Maybe the thought of collaborating, of letting people into your castle, is stressful. But God created us to be in community, which means we have to let people into our space. We need to permit some people to get their fingerprints on our crowns. Relax, I'm not saying we need to let people snatch our crowns away from us, but a little adjustment, a little collaboration, is incredibly healthy.

An Enlightened Few

On July 15, 2020, Bari Weiss stepped down from her high-paying role as a writer and editor at the *New York Times*. For most writers, that is a dream job. So why would she quit a dream job? Here's what she said in her resignation letter: "A new consensus has emerged in the press, but perhaps especially at this paper: that truth isn't a process of collective discovery, but an orthodoxy already known to an enlightened few whose job is to inform everyone else."[3]

That quote is worth pausing and thinking about for a second. Journalists are men and women who search for the truth. They investigate, dig, and ask all the questions the rest of us are afraid to know the answers to. But at least at that paper, according to Weiss, investigative journalism had turned into bowing down to a select "enlightened few." The pursuit of truth had turned into blind obedience.

Do you see the danger of homogeneity? From Weiss's perspective, the paper forced everyone to have the same mindset. Higher-ups figured out the message that catered to their audience and refused to deviate. Editors were crushing her for having different ideas, and it was starting to feel like an act of bravery on her part just to go to work and do her job.

When everyone in the room looks, thinks, and acts the same, it becomes way too easy for the "enlightened few" to create all the narratives. Psychologists call this phenomenon *groupthink*. Collaboration is condemned, and the elite make the decisions while discouraging creativity and critical thinking by the rest of the group.

We'll talk more about this in Part Four, but creating a culture where a few select people tell everyone how to think is harmful. Like Weiss, many people are fed up with this way of operation. Change has begun, and it is starting in individual homes. Are you willing to collaborate? Are you ready to let people into your home who don't look like you?

One of my favorite parts about Acts 10 is how many different people are involved in the story. It's not just a story about Peter. If it were, I'm not sure he would've had a change of heart. It's a story about the power of collaboration.

From a young age, my father showed me how beautiful diversity is and how powerful collaboration can be. It's time for us to pass on the same mindset to our families. Because sometimes the best way to break down walls is to invite people to walk through the door.

Consistency

The final key to fighting homogeneity is *consistency*.

The repetition of Peter's rooftop vision is almost painful. He doesn't get it the first time around, so God simply tries again . . . and again. To make matters worse, this story in Acts 10 is happening about ten years after Peter's first sermon and the launching of the church in Acts 2. Peter wasn't brand-new to all of this; he had been following Jesus for more than a decade, and yet he was still struggling to see gentiles as humans worthy of God's love.

Anyone can understand this: Rome wasn't built in a day, and transformation doesn't happen overnight. Racist roots run deep, and finding freedom is a process.

Roaches

When I began attending White Plains High School, I felt like I lived in two different worlds. School days were very different from the rest of my life. But that began to change when I started making friends. The first friend I made was a White guy named Ben. We immediately hit it off, and once I trusted him enough, I told him where I lived and invited him to spend the night. That was a risk because he could've gotten me kicked out of school.

One day after school he jumped on the bus with me and made the journey to the Bronx. I could tell he was nervous, but he was also willing. Within a few minutes of being in my home, he saw a cockroach and panicked. I mean *really* panicked—he tripped out. His family was well-off, and apparently, money protects you from roaches, so I had to explain to him what he was seeing.

We still laugh about that to this day, because we are still great friends. The thing I respect most about Ben is his consistency. The first night may have been a little strange for him, but he kept coming back. Before long, he fell in love with the place. I can't tell you how many weekends he spent with me in the Bronx, walking around my neighborhood, meeting my neighbors, and trying new food. His consistency paid off.

I was even more nervous the first time Ben invited me to his home. It was my first time going to a White person's house since starting at the school, and you better believe I was minding my p's and q's! There weren't many Black people at our school, so I guess I felt like I had something to prove. I wanted to break any negative impressions his family may have had. But it was all in my head; they were a wonderful family, and didn't need me to put on some act. They invited me right in and taught me so much.

If you feel overwhelmed by this chapter, remember that fighting for diversity is a process. We are striving for progress, not perfection. These things take time, and consistency is way more important than completion.

Long-held biases may not change overnight. However, God is always laying a sheet in front of us. We have a constant invitation to rise and see the world the way God designed it. Every day is a new opportunity to get up and kill the prejudices that keep us from loving everyone and making disciples of all nations.

But the key is consistency, so keep learning, keep reaching out, keep surrounding yourself with diversity. Keep going!

Your Turn

Now it's your turn to do the same thing. Today is the perfect day to invite diversity inside your home. Don't fall into the trap of feeling like you have to change everything overnight; that will only overwhelm you. Instead, take one step today by inviting one person or family who doesn't look like you over for dinner. And don't worry too much about roaches. You don't have to get the exterminator over to your home before you invite people inside. I'm speaking metaphorically, of course. Your home isn't always going to be put together perfectly, but that's the point. Let people see your true self!

Don't put any pressure on it—the win is simply extending the invitation and enjoying the evening. If it goes well, why not see if it can become a monthly thing. You never know when a simple meal is going to turn into a lifelong friendship, or a simple act of kindness is going to have a ripple effect that long outlives your life!

When I look back on my life, I attribute my success to the people who were willing to step up and lead by example along the way. My dad modeled that our home could be an outpost for the United Nations, simply by bringing friends around who didn't look like us. At the church, everyone refers to my father as the Chief of Staff. To be fair, that's how he refers to himself. And for clarity, he's not even on the payroll. He just knows who he is and what he brings to the table, and he does so with *confidence, calmness, collaboration*, and *consistency*.

Today, we get to see the fruit. We still have a long way to go, but my daughters get to grow up in a diverse church surrounded by lots of different people who all love and respect them. My kids go to just as many parties at the homes of atheists as bat mitzvahs for their Jewish friends. By the way, it's customary to send forty dollars with your kids to each bat mitzvah, so around the time my girls were thirteen, my wife and I nearly went bankrupt. We just about started our own diversity campaign by telling them they either had to get more non-Jewish Latino, Black, and brown friends or had to get jobs.

My friend Scott Sauls says, "Instead of creating dividing walls, Jesus breaks down dividing walls." We've seen that happen over and over again in our lives because sometimes the best way to break down walls is to invite people to walk through the door.

You can do the same thing with your home!

Before you move on to the next chapter, talk to your spouse or roommates and send out one dinner invitation to a person who doesn't look like you.

Mr. Koch's compassionate conversations taught me how to be comfortable around a person who doesn't look, dress, or act like me.

Ben's willingness to spend time in the Bronx, learning about roaches, changed the trajectory of both of our lives. By the way, he ended up marrying a beautiful Black woman. And yes, I take some credit for that.

And of course, I would not be where I am today if it weren't for the risk Angelo took to provide me with an opportunity to study in a school where I could thrive and flourish.

Our actions matter. They send out ripple effects into the world. You have no idea how far little acts will go, even the things that don't feel like a big deal. People are watching. You have an influence—your home matters. Get up, get in the game, fight for diversity, and remember: you never know just how far a few free slices of pizza will go.

Take Some STEPS

*To step toward your destiny, you have to
step away from your security.*

—CRAIG GROESCHEL

JOHN SIEBELING

Some kids' first job is a paper route or a lawn-mowing business, but mine was in my father's laboratory, washing equipment used by his burgeoning science students. I may have been too young to explain the periodic table to you, but I had firsthand experience washing those elements off Petri dishes, test tubes, beakers, and other lab utensils during the summer.

My father was a professor at God's favorite university, Louisiana State University—my alma mater and the 2019 NCAA national football champions! Wayne hates it when I gloat about our football team, but while I'm not proficient in science like my dad, I am good with stats, and the last I checked, New York hasn't won an NCAA football championship in years. I've been praying for my brother—that his state would invest in some sports science soon!

As a ten-year-old, I felt like a big shot getting to work on LSU's campus. But I don't mean to romanticize the job. The atmosphere was a treat, but the work was terrible. While other kids were sleeping in, watching cartoons, and enjoying their summer vacations, my dad and I were leaving the house at 6 a.m. We'd get to the lab before the sun was up, and I'd trudge over to the sink, where I was always greeted by a sink full of residue-laden glassware from scientific experiments the day before. That's a tough wake-up call. It smelled like sewer sludge. Then I'd get busy, scrubbing dishes all morning at the lucrative rate of one dollar an hour (it turns out, my dad was just as good at economics as he was at science).

The ministry work I do these days is also dirty work, because we spend our days helping restore messy lives. But I'm telling you, this job in my dad's lab may have been messier. I guess God was preparing me.

The work was tough, but the company was amazing. The best thing about universities is they bring in people from all around the world. My dad's grad students were some of the brightest minds from just about every country in the world, and since I was doing their dirty work for them, they loved me.

Laboratories are rooms equipped for scientific experiments and research. Little did I know that my first job would immerse me in a metaphorical laboratory where I would get to observe the power of a diverse classroom.

I watched people of all skin hues working together. Some had accents that I wasn't acquainted with growing up in Baton Rouge. They were a nice complement to some of the Southern drawls and Cajun-peppered accents I was accustomed to. I saw the power of collaboration and the hard work that goes into finding a solution with people who had different customs and worldviews but surrendered them to meet an objective. All of us had a part to play, even little old me, the dishwasher.

There was a science that I observed back then that became a formula for me throughout the rest of my life: *a diverse group of people, plus a welcoming environment that emphasizes working together, plus a mission or a common goal, equals success.* I may not have left that summer job seeking a science degree, but I feel like I stepped out with a diploma in human science.

The recent pandemic of racism in our times has lobbed us into a national discussion, but even more so into a national lab. In fact, we may be living and working through one of the most significant social experiments of our time. We are working with potentially catastrophic materials (tradition, long-held biases, political allegiances) that need to be handled with care so that we don't continue to experience explosions.

If I learned anything during my brief utensil-washing stint in my dad's lab, it's that science has a methodology. There are steps one has to take to arrive at a solution, and over the years, I've worked on a few steps that I think can help us create diverse communities and avoid burning down our labs.

I consider myself a "list guy." In our monthly podcast, *Leadership in Black and White*, Wayne and I joke that I bring the lists and he brings the alliterations. But I can't help it; I love culling things down into actionable STEPS.

So that's what I've done. In this chapter, I'm giving you the five STEPS that will be a guide to help you build diversity into your community. Here are the five STEPS:

Speak up
Take Personal Responsibility
Educate Yourself
Pray
Start Building Diversity in Your Relationships

Now, I'm more of a practitioner than an expert; this list is by no means the ultimate cure for racism. But what these STEPS will help you do is limit that bacteria-like influence that racism produces.

Information informs, but action transforms—so fight the urge to fly through this list. We are calling these STEPS because we actually want you to apply them to your life. Read each one, and then take us up on the challenge before moving on to the next one!

Step #1: Speak Up

I've devoted most of my life to public speaking in some form or another and have had the privilege of speaking to audiences and leaders around the world. But even with as much talking as I've done, often on very tough subjects, talking about race is one area in which I double down my efforts to prepare and try to be very clear, because I've seen how some conversations can blow up in your face if you don't proceed with caution.

Think about how many people have lost their influence with one tweet.

New York Times writer Tim Kreider coined the term "outrage porn" to explain what he regards as our culture's tendency to be easily offended and even search for more things to be offended by.

Words are dangerous. We have to be careful with them. Like a scientist in a lab who has to monitor which chemicals get mixed together, certain words, combined with unchecked emotion, can become toxic, if not explosive. You can have fewer than a hundred followers on a social media platform, and before you know it, 280 characters go viral and ruin your career and your character.

But that doesn't give us an excuse to stay silent.

Words can also be incredibly healing. Scary as it may sound, we promote what we stay silent about, so we have a responsibility to speak up.

We'll talk about what this means in the context of social media in Chapter 11, but first, we need to spend some time focusing on what speaking up looks like in the context of relationships. And to do that, we need safe settings to practice.

One of the things I loved about working in a laboratory when I was young is that it was a safe place to experiment. We need spaces where we can learn to speak up and use our voices in a contained environment.

In the wake of George Floyd's death, Leslie, Wayne, and I hosted a lunch with a few African American staff members at our church. We wanted to create a safe space for people to speak openly about how they were handling the craziness.

The goal of the lunch was to let the staff members speak while we listened.

What I learned that day wasn't just eye-opening; it was soul-expanding. I fought back tears the entire lunch as I listened to my teammates share their pain and struggles.

One of the women on our team told us that only one White co-worker had spoken up and asked her how she was doing during all the riots and protests.

Thank God for that one friend.

As her pastor, I wish a hundred people had reached out to her. But as we all know, having one person take the time to check in is a million times better than not having anyone reach out. There's a good chance that the people who didn't reach out thought that one conversation was insignificant—but nothing could be further from the truth.

If you've ever felt unqualified to reach out to a hurting friend of another race, let me free you up a little: *empathy* is more important than *eloquence*. You aren't going to get it perfect, but don't let the fear of saying the wrong thing stop you from saying anything at all. You don't have to say anything tweet-able or overtly poignant; when someone is hurting, that person just needs you to empathize. Stop feeling like you have to be an expert scholar on all racial problems before you jump in and have conversations. People need our questions more than our answers. Your presence in people's lives is more important than your solutions.

We will make mistakes. I sure have. I've had to apologize to people for some of the words I've said. Whether we say things out of innocence or ignorance, we can't let those embarrassing moments stop us from speaking out against injustice. If you can make your voice heard in a way that is peaceful, thoughtful, and most important, godly, then you should do so.

Challenge: There are people in your life who need to hear from you, so it's time to open your hands and take a tangible step. Reach out to one person today who doesn't look like you and do three things:

1. Check in with them.
2. Encourage them.
3. Pray for them.

Show that person you care about them. You can give them a call, text them, write them a letter, meet them for coffee, or whatever method works for you. Never underestimate how far asking someone how they are holding up will go. You never know—it may be the exact thing they need today.

Do not discount yourself. People listen to you—the little things you say and do create significant changes in their lives. Just reach out and remind them that you are in their corner!

Step #2: Take Personal Responsibility

When I was in Bible School, my teacher told my class one day that 98 percent of us would not fulfill our calling because we would be too afraid to leave home. That line always stuck with me, because although moving to Kenya and then Memphis was scary, Leslie and I were always up for the challenge. The most significant opportunities are always cloaked in challenge; they just need to be unveiled. Twenty-five years later, I'm so glad I decided to launch and lead a diverse church.

At our church, the entire staff takes personal responsibility to help carry the weight of creating diversity. One day, a member of our staff, who is African American, was giving another pastor a tour of our newly finished broadcast campus. The other pastor asked our team member, "So how do you submit to a White pastor?"

It goes to show how much of an anomaly our church was and the still ever-present implications we have to wrestle with today. Thankfully, our pastor disarmed the question in a way that brought openness and not opposition.

One of the reasons I felt so emotional during that luncheon we hosted for our staff was because I listened to how my team members defended me as their pastor in my absence. Diversity isn't just something we talk about; it's something our staff takes personal responsibility for.

I have watched people leave our church and be very outspoken on social media because they don't like how much we talk about certain issues. I can't tell you how much it hurts to see people distort what you've said or disagree with your position. But my job is not to win a popularity contest; my job is to take personal responsibility for the injustice that I see. I love people so much that their criticisms can trigger me emotionally. However, it's not my job to keep everyone happy; it's my job to keep us moving forward.

Watching our African American team members' spiritual maturity while they defend the culture of our house is moving to me. As my wife, Leslie, put it, hearing their grace-filled responses and seeing the strength of their characters led to some of the holiest and most sacred moments she's ever observed.

In the process of navigating open-handed conversations about race, we may not always get it right. When we miss it, it's tempting to try to pass the buck, but the reality is, we need to own our failures and commit to doing better next time.

Blame is one of the great enemies of unity. For as long as we all refuse to take personal responsibility for our current circumstances, we won't make any progress. There's an old saying, "When you point one finger, three fingers point back at you."

Try it.

Your index finger may be pointing at someone else, but your middle, ring, and pinky fingers are all blaming yourself. It's sort of cheesy, but it's true. When you blame someone else or something else, you disempower your freedom by giving all the power to that other person or thing. If I blame Wayne for my unhappiness (and I usually do if he makes unnecessary comments about my beloved LSU Tigers), I will never be happy until he does something to cheer me up. I still haven't gotten him to wear any LSU merch, which would bring me so much joy! But my happiness is not his responsibility—it's mine. Until I am ready to own it, I will never be happy.

Taking responsibility for racial reconciliation is one of the most important and liberating things you can do. When we acknowledge where we are, we can begin taking steps toward where we want to be. Will you join me in taking personal responsibility for the systematic oppression of Black people in our country?

If you will, we can start to take the necessary steps forward and make a huge difference. The result will be individual freedom and collective progress.

By the way, we still use the word *reconciliation* because it is a biblical word. If the phrase *racial reconciliation* makes you uncomfortable, we aren't trying to suggest there was ever a time of harmony between Black and White people in our nation. Instead, we are saying Jesus reconciled our fractured relationship with God and invites us to work to do the same with each other (2 Cor. 5:18–20).

Challenge: Grab your journal and a pen and spend a few minutes taking an honest look at how you've approached diversity in your life by answering these questions:

If you do not have a diverse circle of friends, why?

Because of your parents?

Because of your hometown?

Because of the demographics of your school, work, or church?

All of those things play a part in your current situation, but at the end of the day, you have to be willing to take *personal responsibility* for your social circle. Once you realize this, you'll start to notice every time you try to shift the blame to external factors.

Step #3: Educate Yourself

These days we don't have any excuse to be uneducated about race. It's easy to criticize previous generations for how they handled race relations, and there is a ton to criticize. But let's also remember they didn't have as many resources readily available to them. That's not an excuse for them; it's a warning for us. We won't have the luxury of telling our grandchildren that we "didn't know," because the information is all around us.

Let's just take books, for example. We are spoiled with the amount of amazing literature out there on this topic. Too often, however, instead of opening a book, we are clenching our fist around the remote and letting the talking heads on our favorite news media outlets tell us what we want to hear.

The only way to excel in education is to continue diving into books like this one. And don't just read people who confirm your beliefs; think critically about and interact with thoughts and opinions that are different from yours.

I picked up a book recently by an author I don't see eye to eye with. After a few pages, I almost put it down. It's not easy to read someone you disagree with, especially if you're passionate about the subject. You'll notice every wrong assumption that person makes, and you'll feel like they're not representing your side well. And for good reason, because they probably aren't.

The author immediately got me riled up, and admittedly, I had to put the book down for a while. But right as I was about to put it back on the shelf, I stopped myself.

If I listen exclusively to voices that agree with me, what am I going to learn? How am I going to grow?

By the way, this feels like a great time to say thank you for not putting this book back on the shelf! Or, if you're dusting it off because we did upset you, welcome back.

The quickest way to dishonor our commitment to advancing racial equality is to stop learning. And when someone recommends a book to you, especially if that person is a different race than you, remember that is a massive opportunity to have an open-handed conversation with them. If you don't have time, make time. Not doing that is like God lobbing you a softball right over the plate and you deciding not to swing. I know we are all busy—trust me, I have plenty of other things to do—but we have to keep reading, learning, and engaging.

I swallowed my pride and kept on reading. And I'm so glad I did. The author made some brilliant observations. Did I agree with everything? No. Not at all. But that doesn't mean I should discount that author entirely. Here's a statement you may not want to hear: *some of the smartest people in the world disagree with you.*

I've heard it said, "Show me your friends, and I'll tell you who you are." That's true, but we should add, "Show me your books, and I'll see how you think."

I have not arrived. I am still learning. Like you, I have to juggle multiple priorities, but I make time for books because I am convinced that leaders are readers. I attribute the successes I've had to a culmination of years of reading articles and books and talking with and learning from incredibly intelligent people. Keep going. Walking across a stage to receive a diploma is a great feeling, but the truth is, your education is never done.

Challenge: Pick one new resource to dive into after you finish this book. And for bonus points, find someone from a different walk of life to go through that resource with you.

Step #4: Pray

At the beginning of 2020, I felt led to lead our church in a year of prayer. What I didn't realize at the time is we were gearing up for one of the most politically polarizing and racially explosive years I've ever experienced.

I don't want to sound trite, and I realize that saying we have to pray can make me come across as Captain Obvious, but I mean this: prayer is essential in bringing about unity, and unity is the secret to ending racism. Could it be that's why Jesus prayed for unity three times in his prayer in John 17?

I am a pastor, not a politician or a social activist; however, you could make the case that I'm called to do a bit of both (more on that later). As a spiritual leader, my field is the soul. I focus on the spiritual, and I believe at their core, racism, prejudice, bigotry, and oppression are sins. We have a spiritual problem on our hands, and spiritual problems require spiritual solutions. I learned much about cleaning dirty utensils as a kid, and that's exactly what prayer does: it washes our hearts and cleanses our souls.

A Place We've Never Been

Remember leading before COVID-19? Leadership has always had its challenges, but when the pandemic hit, everything about leadership changed. I mean, we used to have somewhat predictable patterns in our lives (and restaurant experiences), but COVID-19 fundamentally shifted the way the world works. And then the pandemic of racism reoriented how we lived together as a human race.

I've been leading a local church for twenty-five years now, but this is a place I've never been. I have more questions about leadership, community, and reaching our city than I ever have. I have felt inadequate, and quite honestly, there have been a few days I've considered submitting my dishwasher résumé to the University of Memphis to see if they'd have me.

Fortunately, I'm not the first person to lead in a crazy season, and neither are you.

The book of Joshua tells the story of God taking the Israelites into the promised land. After forty years of wandering, they were excited to finally enter it; however, they were also nervous. The promised land was a place they'd never been to before, and many obstacles were standing in their way. We all know that feeling.

Joshua didn't have a road map; he had to rely on a different type of vision. Watch how Joshua instructs them:

> *When you see the ark of the covenant of the* LORD *your God, and the Levitical priests carrying it, you are to move out from your positions and follow it. Then you will know which way to go, since you have never been this way before.*
>
> (JOSH. 3:3-4)

Joshua acknowledged they were approaching new ground, and his solution was to make sure everyone waited for God to go first. That's what prayer does. It reminds you to let God go first and then empowers you to follow once he does. God is on the move, and many of us need to get out of our longstanding positions and follow the leader.

Challenge: Stop for five minutes and pray for two things. First, ask God to continue bringing racial healing and restoration to homes all around the world. Second, pray that God will start with your *household*. Ask God to bring one diverse friendship into your life and give you the boldness to pursue and cultivate that friendship.

Step #5: Start Building Diversity in Your Relationships

I am a White pastor who proudly leads a church that is approximately 60 percent Black, but that didn't happen by accident.

We intentionally put our mission statement in strategic places—something that we started early on:

> One church in many locations—dynamic, Spirit-filled, and diverse—serving people, developing leaders, and impacting generations.

One Sunday during the early years, an African American woman visited our church. At the end of the service, she approached Leslie with our brochure. She pointed at the mission statement and then ran her fingers over the words until she got to "diverse" and then she looked up and said, "I guess *I'm* the diverse."

And she was right.

At that time, we were Spirit-filled, and we were trying to be dynamic, but we certainly weren't diverse. So instead of getting defensive about what was obviously true, Leslie smiled and replied, "Yes, and would you please stay and help us get there?"

One of the best decisions I made was to ask for honesty from a Black friend who was a part of the congregation. I certainly got what I asked for. We went to lunch once a month for years, and he didn't hold anything back. He answered every question I had.

I learned a lot about his life and the things he experienced growing up as a Black man. He told me some heartbreaking stories about profiling that I didn't want to believe at first, but they were true. As hard as it was, I'm thankful I listened, because we developed a great friendship.

But here's the key: I didn't make friends with him so that he could teach me how to build a diverse church. He wasn't a means to an end; his friendship was the end in and of itself.

Don't build relationships with people outside your race just so you can find solutions. Remember, building relationships with people outside our race *is* the solution.

We became friends first, and a natural outcome of our friendship was the ability for me to ask questions about how I could become a better pastor in this area. The order and the motives matter.

If you are a pastor, I can't tell you how important this is for you. When tragedy hits, many of my pastor friends feel pressured to jump straight to the stage and interview someone publicly they don't know privately. And I get it. I understand that pressure. But rapport can't be faked. People can tell if a friendship is legitimate.

During our lunches, my friend helped give me eyes to see things I couldn't have seen on my own. And now I can honestly say my life is richer because I've enjoyed close relationships with people of color. We laugh big, we cry hard, we serve together, and we learn from each other. We also gain a lot of weight because we all love to eat.

Challenge: Once God answers your prayer and brings an opportunity to have a diverse friendship into your life, it's time to step up to the plate and act. Invite that person to lunch, pick up the tab, ask them about their life, and then just sit back and listen!

Rinse, Wash, Repeat

Every time I finished washing a beaker in my father's laboratory, I felt a moment of accomplishment. But I also knew that feeling wouldn't last. Before long, that beaker would be full of chemicals again, and I would have to repeat the process.

We need to apply that same principle to the five STEPS.

Speak up

Take Personal Responsibility

Educate Yourself

Pray

Start Building Diversity in Your Relationships

And then once you get through all five STEPS—*repeat* the process. That may sound like a lot of work, but before long, you will see your social circle start to change!

Those other kids may have gotten to enjoy their summer vacations, but as a ten-year-old, I inadvertently got a master class in diversity. And while some people continue to sleep in spiritually during these tumultuous times, you have an opportunity to leave the house at 6 a.m., get into your lab (your community, job, and church), and get your hands dirty. It's hard work, but that's what is required to make extremely useful objects clean. Warning: it will be messy, but you'll clean up just fine, and chances are you'll draw a better revenue than I did as a kid. It won't be monetary, but it will be monumental.

Be an Influencer

I am only one, but still I am one. I cannot do everything,
but still I can do something; and because I cannot do
everything, I will not refuse to do something that I can do.

—EDWARD EVERETT HALE

WAYNE FRANCIS

Can anybody have influence? Judging by the trends in our culture that allow even little kids to wield influence on YouTube by just opening toys and commenting on them, apparently the answer is yes.

We live in a world of influencers.

But you already knew that because every time you look at your phone, you see someone with an absurd number of followers setting a new fashion trend, creating a dance, or sharing their opinion about the latest social issue. These days, it feels like I could go viral just by posting a video of myself taking out my garbage.

Then again, I'm probably just jealous. They must be doing something right because some of them, like Kylie Jenner, make more than a million dollars every time they post on Instagram. A million dollars, just to post about a product. And companies will gladly write those checks. That's how much impact they have on culture.

We live in a day and age where influence is quantified (and monetized) by followers, likes, and retweets. It's great for the people who can capitalize on it, but it's dangerous for the rest of us. The problem is, humans love to compare themselves to other humans. In a world full of influencers, it's easy to feel like we will never make a difference.

But that's a lie. You are an influencer.

You may not be getting paid a million dollars to post a picture of your shoes, but if you are a human being, you have influence. Likes and retweets aside, there are people around you to inspire every day.

You matter. And the people you interact with do too.

If we want to work toward a diverse future of unity and reconciliation, we need to know how to use our influence because the conversations we have with people matter.

Racial healing will not come from one perfect post; it will be the culmination of millions of conversations, and you are responsible for some of those. No matter who you are, or how expansive your reach is, you have a part to play.

You are an influencer.

The Unlikely Hero (Part 1)

One of my favorite stories about influence is tucked away in 2 Kings 5. It's a story about a man named Naaman, a prominent commander in the Aramean Army, but the unlikely heroes of the story are all nameless. Technically, they wouldn't ever be able to get an ad sponsorship because their identities are shrouded by anonymity.

Naaman was highly respected and admired for his elite military rank and status. But as quickly as we find out about his power, privilege, and prestige, we also learn about his problem. Naaman had leprosy.

In scripture, leprosy is a portrait of sin and a person's true spiritual condition without God. Aside from being painful, leprosy was a heinous disease that caused the skin to develop lesions, affected the nervous system, and even impaired eyesight.

Picture psoriasis, but on steroids!

In those days, people thought leprosy was highly contagious, so they forced people with the disease to quarantine themselves. Anytime they came near a healthy community, they had to shout, "Unclean!"

Today, it's easier to empathize with how hard that must've been. If COVID-19 has taught us anything, it's how vital community and human touch are. Imagine if you had to shout "I have COVID-19!" every time you left your house.

Everyone would flee.

Leprosy was even worse than that. Naaman's dignity was in danger; he was gearing up for permanent social distancing. The truth is, sickness doesn't care about prestige. To this day, disease still takes the lives of the rich and famous. From Steve Jobs to Bob Marley, all the power in the world can't shield you from illness. Sickness is not agnostic to prestige.

However, help came from the most unlikely source. One of Naaman's slaves was a girl from Israel. Of course, she didn't apply for her job; it was thrust upon her when the Aramean Army captured her. We don't know much about this girl, but one thing is clear: there was a social stratification, a class order, a structure that made people unequal.

One day, she noticed Naaman's leprosy. Now, maybe you are more righteous than I am, but if the guy oppressing me were sick, I'd be tempted to do a touchdown dance and celebrate. But what's shocking is this enslaved girl had enough compassion to tell Naaman's wife about a prophet back in Israel named Elisha who could heal him.

Naaman's wife jumped at the opportunity, which makes sense because she must have been even more desperate for a cure than Naaman. Forgive the lens I read the Bible through, but I picture her like one of those characters we'd see on reality TV, *The Real Housewives of Syria*. "My husband used to be so handsome, but I've got to tell you, there ain't a dermatologist in Syria that can work on that skin. There isn't enough salt in all the sea to rub off some of those scales. If this doesn't get cleared up, we may not get invited to parties anymore; we may need to cancel our family painting—we are falling apart!"

If you are looking for that verse in the Bible, you won't find it. But let's be honest—discovering a cure for her husband was in her best interest.

The shocking part about this story is that the help came from the *nameless* enslaved girl. "Influence" typically isn't the first word that comes to mind when you think of someone who is enslaved. This poor girl was certainly not living out her dream. However, instead of making excuses and pointing the finger at her oppressor, she pointed her oppressor to a solution. She pointed her enemy to the answer.

For those of us who are highly melanated, that is a tough pillow to swallow. And yes, I said "pillow" because pointing oppressors to solutions can feel more like attempting to swallow a pillow than a pill!

And yet, that is the call in scripture. You. Yes, you, person of color, have the unique opportunity to offer hope to someone afflicted with the sin of racism. Some may call that cowardice. I'm not suggesting that people of color shouldn't speak out against injustice; I'm just saying that we could see more change happen if we keep pointing people to an answer beyond ourselves.

Here's the deal: suffering exists. And some people will find themselves in the position of being disproportionately impacted by that suffering. But, *look* at this girl: through her submission (albeit involuntary) to her master and her service to his wife, despite being uprooted from her family and home, she still thought of someone else. I find that utterly compelling. If we know the cure, we have to keep telling people about it.

She's the hero of the story, and we don't even know her name.

Influence doesn't have to be about numbers, reach, or getting paid. As we will talk about in the next chapter, there's nothing wrong with those things. But let's not forget that some of the most influential people in history didn't have TikTok.

Influence is more about respect than reach.

Are you willing to cheer a co-worker on toward a promotion, even if that means you may not get one yourself?

Are you willing to sit down with someone who looks down

on you for the color of your skin and have a civilized conversation with that person?

Are you willing to fight for someone who won't fight for you?

Are you willing to point your oppressor to the solution?

Are you willing to "love your enemies and pray for those who persecute you" (Matt. 5:44)?

That is influence.

The Great Commission

At this point, you may feel a little intimidated or overwhelmed.

Take a breath. Using your influence is an ongoing and life-long process. It's a lifestyle, a daily choice.

Jesus gave his disciples a command before ascending to his Father. He told them, "Therefore go and make disciples of all nations, baptizing them in the name of the Father and of the Son and of the Holy Spirit, and teaching them to obey everything I have commanded you. And surely I am with you always, to the very end of the age" (Matt. 28:19–20).

The initial reading of this feels forceful: "Go!" It has an urgent tone to it, but when you study the word translated as *go* in the original Greek, it can be seen to mean *as you go*. As you go about your day, make disciples. As you go for your venti caramel soy latte, make disciples. As you go for a workout, make disciples. It's about doing it in your day-to-day rhythm.

Influence works best when it's natural.

You are on this earth for a reason. God wired you how he wired you and placed you where he placed you for a reason. So relax, just live your life, and as you go, look for opportunities to use your influence.

You don't have to do everything.

You can't do everything.

But you can do something.

Don't try to fix thousands of years of systemic racism on your own. Just focus on what you focus on.

If you are a teacher, you have a classroom full of future leaders to inspire. Focus on being the best teacher you can be and find creative ways to raise a new generation of kids who are not intimidated by conversations about race.

If you run a company, you have opportunities to influence all of your employees and customers. Look for creative ways to inspire and create space for healthy conversations.

If you are a student, you have an entire school filled with fellow students eager to learn and grow.

As you go to the mall, use your influence.

As you take your kids to soccer practice, use your influence.

As you go to your office, use your influence.

As you hang out with your friends, use your influence.

Everywhere you *look*, there are opportunities to influence people. You don't have to change everything about your life; just focus on what you focus on, and *as you go*, use your influence. This takes some practice, but fortunately, every day is another opportunity to get more reps as you go.

I know this topic of influence can feel overwhelming, so to keep things simple, I boiled this chapter down to a list of three items. Now, I know in the last chapter John said he's the list guy and I'm the alliteration guy, so you'd better believe everything on my list starts with the same letter. Here are the Three *L*'s of Influence:

Listen

Look

Learn

(And make sure you read to the end, because there may be
a bonus fourth *L*.)

As You Go . . . LISTEN

The starting point for influence is learning how to *listen*.

Some of the best conversations I've ever had happened
around a fire. A few months ago, Classy and I went over to
some friends' house for dinner. Afterward, we sat around the
fire pit in their backyard for a few hours, talking about our
country's racial tensions. All I did was ask one question, and
we were off to the races.

During the conversation, they said some things that came
across as unsettling, but the more we talked, the more we
realized their words were just uninformed. Classy and I felt
like we had climbed in a time machine and traveled back several decades to the first time we started engaging in the race
conversation.

But all we did was listen.

To be honest, there were moments when I wanted to pull
my hair out. Everything inside me wanted to interrupt and
interject. But we love them, and we understood that what they
needed was a safe space to process and learn. So instead, we
just kept *listening*. And later that night, while we were dozing
off to sleep, we got this text from them: "Thanks for listening.
Let's do it again soon."

That's what influence is all about; their lives transformed
that night, and all we did was listen. As counterintuitive as
it sounds, *listening* is more important than reacting; influence
starts with your ears before it moves to your mouth.

James, a pillar of the early church, wrote, "My dear brothers and sisters, take note of this: Everyone should be quick to listen, slow to speak and slow to become angry" (James 1:19). In a world that is *slow* to listen and *quick* to become angry, you have an opportunity to make an impact on someone's life simply by being willing to *listen* and understand. Everyone you meet is fighting a battle. Everyone has hurts, habits, and hang-ups holding them back, so when they start expressing them, just let them do that. The worst thing you can do at that moment is to interrupt with your opinions. Even if you disagree with what they are saying, just let them express themselves.

The next time you enter into a conversation with someone, consciously remind yourself to really listen to what they have to say. Practice being fully present by fighting the urge to formulate your response while they are talking. You'll be amazed at how quickly they will start opening up about things and experience healing when you create space for them to process their pain.

I've sat down with several counselors over the years. Counselors are essentially professional listeners, and they always emphasize the importance of active listening. One great technique is to repeat back to the other person what you believe you heard—for example, using a line like "Is it correct that when you said _____, you meant _____?" Doing this forces us to pay attention, breaks down any internal biases, and lets the other person know that we are actually present with them.

Learning to *listen* is like putting your finger on the pulse of culture. So if you want to have influence, learn to *listen* as you go.

Are you a good listener? Here are a few questions to ask yourself:

Am I listening to learn, or am I listening to respond?

Do I care about the person as much as I care about the problem?
Will I be content even if I don't get any credit for leading them
to a solution?

As You Go . . . LOOK

Looking at someone is a sign of respect, a way to communicate that you care about what someone is saying. We've all been to those lunches with someone who is staring at their phone the whole time, subconsciously throwing up an invisible wall across the table. Don't be that person. If you want to influence people, learn to *look* at them. The truth is, there are people to influence everywhere. We just have to learn how to keep our eyes open as we go.

The Unlikely Hero (Part 2)

Naaman made the long journey from Aram to Jerusalem, but when he finally got to Elisha's house, the prophet didn't even come out to speak to him. He sent a messenger instead.

Can you imagine Naaman rolling up to the prophet's house in the finest chariot of the day? The 586 BC chariot while everybody else still had the old 587 BC version. Naaman was probably hoping the prophet would come light some incense, give an incantation, and send him on his way so he could go back to his 4 p.m. meeting about conquering a nearby enemy. I can only imagine what was going through Naaman's mind when Elisha sent out a messenger.

What kind of concierge service is this?

Do you know who I am?

Are you really sending out a courier to talk to me?

I didn't travel all this way to talk to a messenger; I want to speak to the prophet.

Notice the pattern in this story.

The only reason Naaman was there in the first place was because he *listened* to an enslaved girl. His next step was to *look* at a messenger, but he couldn't do it. His power, privilege, and prestige kept him blind to people. He thought he was too important to see the messenger standing right in front of him. Are you starting to see that Naaman's leprosy wasn't the only thing he needed to heal from? And once again, God used a *nameless* messenger to get him there.

Do you ever struggle to *look* at the people standing right in front of you?

One of the biggest mistakes some of my pastor friends make is they want to find easy solutions to racial tension without really *looking* into the problems first. There is nothing wrong with investing money in overlooked communities or bringing a guy like me in to talk to their congregation on a Sunday. Those things are noble and good, but they are also quick fixes that allow us to *overlook* the problem instead of *looking into* it.

How many opportunities to love someone do you miss every day because you aren't keeping your eyes open?

Looking at someone means more than just seeing them; it means actually looking into the things they are saying. Here's a new rule: If you care about someone, learn to care about what they care about. If it's important to them, make it important to you. Be curious about the things they are curious about and passionate about the things they are passionate about.

Today, when you enter into any conversation with someone (especially a conversation with someone who doesn't look like you), consciously tell yourself to *look* at that person. Worry less about what you are adding to the discussion and more about making that person feel seen. You'll be amazed at how interesting people and their passions are when you learn to *look*!

As You Go . . . LEARN

If you want to use your influence, it helps if you have something to say. But to have something to say, you have to be willing to *learn*. In the last chapter, John encouraged us to keep reading. Another great way to learn is to *go*.

One of my favorite things about living in New York is I'll never run out of new experiences. No matter how hard I try, I will never eat at every restaurant, watch every concert, and see every show. It's impossible. There is too much to do.

New experiences teach you new things. Visiting new parts of town, experiencing new cultures, tasting new types of food, and hanging out with people you wouldn't usually spend time with—they are all great teachers. It's one of the enormous benefits of living in a diverse city.

Have you ever noticed your life getting into a rut? You order the same meal from the same restaurant while you have the same conversation with your spouse before you go home and watch the same show.

We are creatures of habit.

But when we get stuck, we stop *learning*. Sometimes God breaks us out of our regularly scheduled programming to teach us something. That's exactly what happened to Naaman.

The Unlikely Hero (Part 3)

Naaman's journey toward healing took him to a place he'd never been to before. After leaving his hometown and traveling all that distance, the messenger told him to wash in the Jordan River. In frustration, Naaman responded, "Are not Abana and Pharpar, the rivers of Damascus, better than all the waters of Israel? Couldn't I wash in them and be cleansed?" (2 Kings 5:12).

That's a fair objection. He traveled all that way just to find out that the solution was to jump into a river that wasn't even as pristine as the rivers he had at home. If a prophet told me the cure was to dip myself in the Hudson River in New York City (a milder version of the Jordan River in those times), I'd be angry, too.

After all, he was trying to *cure* his disease, not *contract* one.

What's going on here? First, Naaman had to drive down to the hood to see the prophet (I don't know if Elisha lived in the hood, but I bet that anything outside of Naaman's community was considered the hood), who had the audacity to not even come outside to meet him, and then without advance notice he was told to go down to the mud bath waters of the Jordan.

Have you ever been guilty of someone presenting a new way for you to grow in this race issue and you scoffed at it, thinking that there had to be a better and less difficult way? Sometimes we can be guilty of seeking easier ways to resolve our leprosy-like condition of racism. We would rather be awash in ease than drenched in the difficulty of submission.

Remember, Naaman's journey to healing was about a lot more than leprosy. God was breaking him out of his old mindsets; but first, he had to break him out of his bubble. Could

God be doing the same thing in your own journey toward becoming an agent of racial healing?

There is power in experiencing new places and meeting new people. Typically, people with hatred or bias toward a people group don't know many of them. The closer we get to people, the more we appreciate them. Having conversations with people who don't look like you or visiting parts of town where they live is one of the most educational experiences you will ever have.

Although there may be rivers in your hometown, sometimes God will bring you to a new one. He may have something to teach you that you couldn't have *learned* back there.

Firsthand experience is valuable.

If you want to increase your influence, you need to *learn*. Don't be afraid to try new things, go to new places, and meet new people. And as you go, *learn*. Expand your horizons and increase your perspective, and then the next time you have a conversation, you'll have something to say.

When the time came for Naaman to wash in the Jordan River, he hesitated again. Even though he'd come this far, a piece of him was still opposed to the whole process. I imagine he was embarrassed; his ego had taken quite a few hits.

But guess who the final unlikely hero is? That's right—one of his nameless servants talks some sense into him, saying, "My father, if the prophet had told you to do some great thing, would you not have done it? How much more, then, when he tells you, 'Wash and be cleansed'!" (2 Kings 5:13).

Here's a modern-day translation of that verse: "Bro, if The Rock would have suggested the Jordan River, you would have already ordered some river water on Amazon and posted a selfie of you dipping in that water with the hashtag #therock cleansingtechniques!"

I love that Naaman's servant felt permission to be honest with him. He didn't just tell his master what he wanted to hear; he told him what he needed to hear. We can honor and still be honest.

And once Naaman is willing to *learn* from a nameless enslaved girl, messenger, and servant, he is finally ready to heal:

So he went down and dipped himself in the Jordan seven times, in accordance with the word of the man of God; and his flesh was restored like the flesh of a little child, and he was clean.

(2 KINGS 5:14, NASB)

He dipped once, and nothing happened, but then he dipped again and again, and eventually, on the seventh dip, he came out of the water completely healed.

That's how it works, isn't it?

Many people I interact with, particularly White leaders, want to get to the solution for racism fast. But remember, slavery in North America lasted hundreds of years. There is no quick fix for healing. It will take a few immersive experiences to get cleansed of the leprous effects of racism.

The *first* conversation you have may not open your eyes.

The *second* movie on racism you watch may not get you to admit that you have privilege.

The *third* diverse dinner you host might not change your mind.

And these first *ten* chapters of this book might not have done it for you yet.

But keep dipping yourself in uncomfortable waters, and eventually, you *will* see change.

Remember Peter hearing a vision three times before he was ready to *listen*? We see something very similar in Naaman's story. One dip wasn't enough to cleanse him of his disease—or wash off years of bigotry, racism, and pride. He had to dip over and over again because change doesn't happen overnight.

Some of your diverse relationships may not click immediately—but don't give up hope. There is a reason that person is the way they are and acts the way they act, so never stop learning about their culture and customs. Be willing to take the time to come to them and *learn* about who they are. The results may not be *immediate*, but if we persevere, the payoff will be *immense*.

In a world full of influencers who get paid for social media posts, we have to remember that true life change happens over time. We are a microwave generation with rotisserie problems. We want harmony to happen the same way a meal happens with Hamburger Helper: add some water, stir, zap it on high for three to five minutes, and voilà.

But harmony doesn't work that way.

It's going to take time.

So as you go, keep *listening*, keep *looking*, and keep *learning*.

Be the Influencer

Let's recap.

Second Kings 5 is a story about a man with privilege, power, and a problem. But the true heroes of the story are a nameless enslaved girl, an anonymous messenger, and an unknown servant.

We don't know their names, but we still talk about their influence. Why? Because history belongs to the humble. Prideful people may make history books, but it's usually for all the wrong reasons. Those who lay down their lives for others, metaphorically and literally, are remembered forever.

I know that some of our readers who are people of color might be tense right now, and I'm hoping our White readers are equally nervous because this is a story that messes with us deeply. It's provocative. All of us can insert ourselves into one part of the story or another. One little enslaved girl catalyzed amazing change in an army commander. One person of privilege, prestige, and power got cleansed because he submitted to a process. Some nameless servants spoke up to somebody who could have fired them or done worse. To me, that's speaking to power and not just relying on a social media post to communicate our positions on race.

Leprosy began within, with an invisible contagion, but then became visible on the skin. Racism starts in our hearts and then shows up in our actions. It's time to wade in new waters.

Wherever you are reading this, you have an opportunity to do the same. You live in a world riddled by racism, off-color jokes, generation bias, and political idolatry. But remember, you are here for a reason.

Remember Dr. Paul Brand, who had the practice of immersing his hands in scalding hot water to ensure that he could still feel the pain and therefore had not contracted leprosy? John and I are hoping the Spirit of God, like immersive fire, is helping you make sure that you still feel deeply for marginalized and *overlooked* people and that you are aware of how to empathize in the fight against racism.

If you want to have influence, it starts with remembering the Three *L*'s of Influence:

Listen: Care enough about people to truly *listen* to what they have to say. Even if you disagree with what they are saying, "everyone should be quick to listen, slow to speak and slow to become angry" (James 1:19).

Look: Get in the habit of actually *looking* at people. See people for who they are, not what they can do for you.

Learn: Be a student of people. Everyone has a unique story that brought them to this moment in their life. Never stop asking them questions and *learning* what makes them who they are.

We are living in a historic moment. People will read about these times in history books. When they do, what type of story will they read?

Will they read about how we had a chance to create change, but never did anything about it? Or will they read about millions of people who all decided to play their part and do what they could do to influence the people right in front of them?

Will they read about how we *listened* to learn, not just listened to respond?

Will they read about how we *looked* at every single person?

Will they read about how we got out of our comfort zones and *learned* about different cultures and people?

History belongs to the humble. Our names may not make the history books, but we can make sure our neglect doesn't either.

You are an influencer. You have a part to play.

We all have a part to play. Let's play it well.

Bonus: As You Go . . . LAUGH

I warned you up top that there may be a bonus word. In Bible School, they taught us to communicate in threes. But I'm a grown man, so how about a fourth *L* for those in the back?

Everyone who knows me knows how much I love to *laugh*. Laughter is a universal language that brings us together. It gives us room to take a deep breath and exhale. Until we start to understand the languages that unite us, like music and laughter, we will have a hard time dealing with each other.

Conversations on race don't have to be tense. Laughter helps us relax.

I recently read a story about a White woman who organized a small group made up entirely of other White women. She was trying to take steps to diversify a bit, so she got excited when a Black woman registered for the group. But she was also nervous; she really wanted to make sure the lady felt right at home, so she reached out beforehand and asked, "Should I refer to you as Black or African American?"

The message made the Black woman smile, and she responded, "I think Margaret will do."

I love that. Sometimes we get so uptight about this subject that we forget basic social cues. Her name is Margaret; just call her by her name.

We need to loosen up a bit. And *laughter* is the perfect way to do that.

Laughter and influence are deeply intertwined. Laughter breaks down barriers and puts people at ease. The Bible says, "A cheerful heart is good medicine" (Prov. 17:22). Like medicine, humor makes everyone feel better. If you want to influence someone, make them *laugh*, and watch what happens.

Pick Your Battles

GUARDRAILS FOR WINNING WITH WORDS

Most of the disputes of the world arise from words.

—WILLIAM MURRAY, LORD MANSFIELD

JOHN SIEBELING

I heard a great joke a while back: "There's a new app that tells you which one of your friends is racist. It's called Facebook."

Like all good jokes, this one is just as haunting as it is hilarious.

We live in a new world. The digital age is here to stay. Every person who wants to say something now has a stage they can stand on to say it, and they don't need to get their message approved by anyone before they share it. Thanks to social media, the entire world is at our fingertips.

At the start of 2020 more than 3.8 billion people used social media. That was about half of the world's population at the time, and the number is increasing by 9 percent every year.[1] For a long time, most people were just jumping on to watch the conversations unfold, but now a growing number of people are jumping in to participate. A 2020 Pew Research Center study showed that around 50 percent of Americans had engaged in some form of political or social-minded activity on social media in the previous year.[2]

Back in the day, crowds gathered in stadiums or coliseums to hear about and discuss social issues, but these days much of the conversation is happening online. TikTok, Twitter, Facebook, and Instagram are the new arenas.

And these arenas have an open mic policy.

Unfortunately, people say some unbelievably mean things to each other when they are hiding behind a screen. Social media makes it way too easy to be a lamb in person but a lion online. And the pain we create with social media is real. When the COVID-19 pandemic hit in 2020, people in the church stopped seeing each other in person for a while. I received phone calls from faithful volunteers who told me they were afraid to come back to church and serve because of the things people on their team were posting online.

It happens more than you think.

In Part Three, we've been learning how we can use our influence to invite diversity into our own *households*. In this chapter, we talk about some guardrails for the conversations we have so our words can be more *helpful* than *hurtful*. We aren't always going to get it right, but these guardrails will be a *guide* and help us avoid some of the common landmines that can blow up into conflict.

Whether we want to admit it or not, a growing percentage of these conversations are now happening online. Social media platforms are pivotal parts of this discussion, so that is our focus. However, all of these guardrails can be applied to every conversation you have. So let's talk about your online presence, because the truth about your timeline is, it really does matter.

Your tweets matter.

Your posts matter.

Your comments matter.

People are watching.

The things you say have a real impact on real people. And while it may be tempting to delete all of our accounts, burn our phones, and bury our heads in the sand, that's not the way forward. As Wayne talked about in the last chapter, we need to use our influence. This chapter is not a call to abandon this gift; it's a call to use it responsibly. But in order to know how to do that, we have to understand the good, the bad, and the ugly sides of social media.

The Good

Social media expands our horizons. It gives us front-row seats to different cultures and customs that interest us. My wife is Italian and loves to follow Italian chefs and people living in Italy. These days she can see and learn so much about Italy without jumping on a plane. Social media allows her to feel connected with her cultural heritage, from our home.

And how amazing is it that we can connect with the people we love, no matter where they live? Grandparents everywhere rejoice that they can watch their grandkids grow up. We used to send pictures via snail mail; now, we just click a button. Thanks to social media, geographical distance is no longer an obstacle standing in the way of connection.

Social media also gives everyone a voice. We'll talk about the ugly side of that in a moment, but before we get there, we can all agree that having a public space to use your voice is a positive thing.

If you have something to say, it helps to have somewhere to say it. Jesus used to stand on a mountain or get in a boat and put out into the water a little way so that his voice would project far enough for thousands of people to hear. I can record a video from my office right now, and the entire world will have access to it in seconds.

I certainly wish Facebook had existed twenty-five years ago when we were planting our church. Posting ads in newspapers was fun and all, but posting on my timeline is cheaper, easier, and way more effective. Social media is a fantastic tool that is here to stay. But as good as it is, some dangers also lurk beneath the surface.

The Bad

Social media can be addicting. Have you noticed?

The next time you are stuck in a line at the grocery store or are waiting for someone to show up to a meeting, pay attention to what you do. Our phones have rewired and retrained our brains to reach for our pockets and check for likes, retweets, and friend requests.

A recent sobering study found that the average internet user spends more than six hours online every day. That's a cumulative 1.25 billion years online this year. And more than one-third of that time will be on social media.[3]

Tristan Harris, a former design ethicist at Google, has been warning us about this for several years. Harris likens our smartphone to having a slot machine in our pocket. He explains how experts strategically designed social media platforms to keep us hooked, giving us just enough rewards and enticing us with the right amount of suspense to keep our eyeballs glued to the screen.

Harris believes these apps were designed this way intentionally because your attention is valuable. The longer you stare at your screen, the more money a company can charge advertisers. And it's all happening at the expense of our attention spans and relationships.

He calls this *human downgrading.*[4]

It's no wonder that the number of people experiencing mental health issues is on the rise. Increased use of Facebook, Snapchat, TikTok, and Instagram is linked with greater loneliness, fear of missing out (FOMO), depression, and body image issues.[5]

This book is about learning to have open-handed, life-giving conversations about *God and race*, but unfortunately, it's tough to have conversations when we can't even stay present with each other in the same room.

The rise of social media has meant the fall of our attention spans and social intelligence. But that's not even the worst of it.

The Ugly

Social media creates distance, and distance distorts our conscience.

When people argue online, they end up saying things they would never say in person. Screens have a way of dehumanizing the people we are talking to. But the recipients of our words are real people.

A few years ago, the coach of the Memphis Grizzlies (our NBA team) started attending our church. A young guy on my staff was excited because he is a huge Grizzlies fan. But the first time he saw the coach in church, he panicked and started wondering whether he had ever talked trash about him on Twitter. This guy is one of the nicest people I know; he is the last person you'd expect to do that, but that's just sports culture.

What's interesting is he never thought twice about critiquing the coach until he started serving next to him in church. Then suddenly, the coach he had seen only on TV became a real human being.

Someone's son.

Someone's dad.

A member of our church.

Distance creates division. Which is why people say things on social media they would never say in person.

That day, this young staff member took a deep dive into all his social media platforms to make sure he deleted everything. By the way, it may be a good time for us to put this book down for a few minutes and do the same thing. It's not about erasing evidence; it's about cultivating compassion and committing to changing the way we talk about people from this day forward. If we want to be history makers, we need to take a few minutes to go back to our past and scrub our timeline.

Can we do that together? Seriously.

If you are embarrassed about what you may find, you'll

make every excuse not to do it, but that's just a sign that you probably should. Just get it done. You'll feel a thousand times lighter afterward.

A recent Pew Research Center study found that 73 percent of adult internet users have witnessed harassment online. Think about how commonplace online harassment must be if the overwhelming majority of internet users have seen it. What's worse is that 40 percent of them admitted they've experienced harassment firsthand.[6]

Those numbers are disturbing, but they aren't shocking. As a pastor, I have a ring-side seat to this fight. I'm shocked by some of the things people post. Social media is polarizing our nation. We'll talk more about what that means for the church in Chapter 13, but first, we need to talk about your rights and your calling.

The First Amendment

Don't I have the right to freedom of speech?

I can hear the voices already. Before we go any further, let's get on the same page. Yes! Of course you have that right. It's one of the beautiful things about this country, and I would never try to take that from you. If you are a citizen of the United States, you have the right to freedom of speech. But Paul reminds us we are also citizens of heaven (Phil. 3:20), which means our calling is to speak life over people and strive toward unity. Just because we have the right to say something doesn't mean we should.

In his first letter to the church in Corinth, Paul writes,

"'Everything is permissible,' but not everything is beneficial" (1 Cor. 10:23, CSB). Even though we have the right to post what we want, our responsibility is to build up.

A few months ago, someone in our church approached me, visibly upset. The night before, this person had seen a post from another person who attends our church that brought them to tears. They couldn't wrap their mind around how someone who hugs them every Sunday could turn around and directly attack their race online.

Do you see the danger here?

That's not beneficial.

And by the way, this happens both ways. I've had Black people come up to me and complain about what a White person is saying and the other way around.

The truth about your timeline is, it really does matter. People are watching. People are listening. Your platform is a gift; it would be wrong to waste it. But with great power comes great responsibility.

The question is: *How do you continue to practice your freedom of speech, and speak out about the things you are passionate about, without hurting people?*

In the second half of the verse, Paul gives us a filter. He says we can know something is beneficial if it builds up and is constructive. As a pastor, let me first say I have no control over people's social media use. But I do want to urge you to pick your battles wisely and make sure your posts are constructive. I can't tell you what or how to post, but if you are serious about racial unity and you feel there is any chance that your post may be misconstrued, I'd highly recommend that you put up these four guardrails.

Guardrail #1: Pray before you post.
Guardrail #2: Pause before you post.
Guardrail #3: Host before you post.
Guardrail #4: Maybe just don't post.

Guardrail #1: Pray Before You Post

The first and most important guardrail is to hit your knees before you hit the post button. When social media first came out, it was just a fun way to communicate with each other, but these days the things we say have real ramifications, which means we should get in the habit of sharing the post with God before we share it with the world. Prayer realigns our will with God's will, so pray before you post, and if you don't feel peace, take a step back and reevaluate not just what you are saying, but also how you are saying it.

Here are three questions to meditate on while you pray:

Does this post promote peace?

Is this post unifying?

Will this post lead to love?

Posting on social media is not just about what we say; it's also about how we say it. You may be right about something, but if you don't communicate it in love, you're wrong. Paul starts his famous chapter about love by writing, "If I speak in the tongues of men or of angels, but do not have love, I am only a resounding gong or a clanging cymbal" (1 Cor. 13:1). Have you ever heard someone try to learn how to play drums? It's not fun. No rhythm. No flow. It's just noise, resounding gongs, and clanging cymbals.

Without love, your post is the same thing—just noise.

And trust me, we have more than enough of that, so pray before you post.

Guardrail #2: Pause Before You Post

Whether we are posting or responding to a comment, it's good to get in the habit of hitting the pause button before the post button. One way to do this that I've found effective is to take three big, deep breaths. While you breathe, ask yourself these three questions:

Am I reacting emotionally?

Is this post intended to help or to hurt?

Does this post disciple or divide?

While social media is a great tool, it's a horrible place to vent. Pause and ask yourself if you really want to post or if you are just looking for a place to process your pain. Venting isn't bad; it's a normal part of being a human. I'd never tell someone to stuff their feelings down or pretend they aren't there. But social media is not the place for it. Get a friend, or a counselor, or a dog, but please don't work out your emotions on such a public and permanent forum.

Take a deep breath and make sure you aren't acting impulsively.

By the way, if you find yourself wanting to post about something over and over again, that can be a great indicator of a pain pocket in your heart. Again, I'm not trying to pull the rug out from under you. I'm glad you are passionate, and I want you to use your voice, but let's not mistake passion for pain. Are you really passionate about the subject, or do you need to heal from the pain it causes?

Quick, emotionally-driven posts are typically a good indicator that it's the latter.

Here's what Proverbs, or "Ancient Twitter" (as Wayne calls it), says about this subject: "Too much talk leads to sin. / Be sensible and keep your mouth shut" (Prov. 10:19, NLT). Ask yourself if this post will be productive in the discipleship process. If it is, great. If it's not, it's better to keep your mouth shut.

Guardrail #3: Host Before You Post

A lot of the arguments and polarizing content filling the World Wide Web today comes from people who are uninterested in meeting with or talking to anyone who has a different opinion. A lot of them are so uninterested in actual human interaction that they keep their identity hidden. We call these people keyboard warriors, because they talk a big game, but they aren't living it out.

Guardrail #3 will help you avoid falling into that trap.

Before you post about a social issue, host a conversation. If you are posting something about a racial issue, invite someone of a different skin color over for dinner, and ask that person their thoughts. Make sure you're living out the thing you are posting about. You'll be amazed at how having personal relationships changes your perspective on problems.

This guardrail forces you to answer the question, "Would I say this to someone's face?"

Wayne and I help each other with this all the time. We both acknowledge that we have a limited perspective and need each other's opinions. He'll notice how I phrase certain things that I would never even think to address, and vice versa. We have to be humble enough to receive criticism from each other, because as the writer of Ecclesiastes says, "Two are better than one" (Eccles. 4:9).

Are you willing to host a conversation before you post your opinion?

This guardrail takes more time, but it's worth it. If you don't have time, make time. Hosting conversations leads to relationships. And when we have diverse friendships, we are going to think about our friends before flippantly saying things online. You'll find that hosting the conversation is often even more fruitful than anything that comes out of the post.

Before you hit post, take time to host.

Guardrail #4: Maybe Just Don't Post

How many times have you said something, and while it was on the way out, wished you could reel it back? In the heat of the moment, we say things we don't mean, and we hurt people in the process.

A few months into COVID-19, I had a moment of frustration. I think we all had at least one of those. For a while, everyone was terrified that the virus could spread easily from touching surfaces, so everyone was furiously wiping down their groceries when they brought them home. But then the Centers for Disease Control and Prevention (CDC) came out with a report about how that wasn't true, and I got frustrated. It felt like we were getting different (and contradicting) information every day. And it was causing so many people pain and anxiety in the process.

I was on vacation with my family when the story came out, and instead of being present with them, I shifted my attention to creating a snarky post. My wife and my daughter both told me not to, but I couldn't help myself.

Looking back, I was just frustrated, especially since every passing report made meeting together as a church more complicated.

I posted it but later regretted my decision. Especially when I found out one of the pastors on my staff was asked a question about that post during his Life Group that forced him to stand up and defend me.

Honestly, it was very mild, but it wasn't helpful.

Sometimes it seems like everything we need to know we learned in kindergarten: *if you don't have anything nice to say, don't say anything at all.*

If you find yourself hesitating as you go through these ground rules, remember, you don't have to post. Trust me, I know the pressure to speak up about racial injustice. People will tell you you're being complicit if you wait too long before speaking up, especially if you are a pastor. I understand where they are coming from, but sometimes that burden is too heavy to bear. Besides, you are never going to make everyone happy, so take some pressure off yourself.

Yes, your voice matters.

Yes, you have something to say.

But the sobering truth is, the world will get on just fine without your opinion. As Ancient Twitter says, "Even fools are thought wise if they keep silent, / and discerning if they hold their tongues" (Prov. 17:28).

That verse says it all.

For some of us, shutting up is the most helpful thing we can do. You don't have to post. Pick your battles wisely. If you aren't feeling peace about it, just say no.

How to Spark a Revolution

At this point, it may feel like I am against social media, but I'm really not. My intention is not to discourage you from posting; it's simply to put up some guardrails to help you have even more reach.

George Floyd's tragic death was a terrible event in US history, but it sparked a movement. Why? Because a seventeen-year-old named Darnella Frazier had the sense to pull out her phone and capture the entire thing on film. And then, she had the courage to utilize her platform to create change.

Within minutes, people from all around the world were crying, mourning, and getting justifiably angry. It started a movement, and the rest is history.

That's the beauty of social media. When we use it wisely, it creates change. The digital age is exposing so many ugly things that used to get swept under the rug. Things that have always been true are now in the light for everyone to see. Will Smith said it best: "Racism is not getting worse, it's getting filmed."[7]

That wouldn't happen without social media.

Social media is a fantastic tool and will continue to be a necessary ally as we move toward racial healing. When used correctly, it can bear a ton of excellent fruit. Your timeline is powerful. But before you add to it, take the time to

Pray before you post.

Pause before you post.

Host before you post.

And potentially, delete what you have and start over.

Although it may take time, it will be time well spent.

If you still feel at peace, by all means, post. Don't diminish your voice. You have something to say; use your voice and say it well, because the truth about your timeline is, it really does matter. Just remember what the Bible says, "Don't use foul or abusive language. Let everything you say be good and helpful, so that your words will be an encouragement to those who hear them" (Eph. 4:29, NLT).

HOST A MULTICULTURAL DINNER

Your voice matters. What you do in response to Part Three can change the way your *household* approaches the race conversation for generations to come. To end this section, your final assignment is to *host a multicultural dinner.*

One of the best ways to invite diversity into your home and enter into conversations about racial unity is to find common ground. Food is one of the best ways to do this. It doesn't matter who you are or where you are from—we all need to eat. Food brings everyone together (Jesus knew this and constantly used this strategy).

Reach out to friends and neighbors (preferably ones from different parts of the world) and invite them over for dinner. Encourage everyone to bring their favorite dish that represents their culture. Before you eat, give everyone a couple of minutes to present their dish and explain why it means so much to them.

Then pray for the meal, thank God for the beauty of different cultures, and set everyone loose to eat. You'll be amazed at how quickly and easily everyone enters into conversations about other cultures when delicious food is the starting point!

Don't let this assignment stress you out—it's intended to be fun. You don't need to invite your entire neighborhood. Start small and extend the invitation to a few friends the first time. If it goes well, you can get a little bolder the next time around. You never know: one dinner may turn into a new tradition for your community.

PART FOUR

House of God

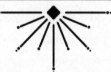

Racial healing begins in our hearts. In Part Two, we learned how to put in the hard work to empathize with everyone and process our pain. In Part Three, we shifted our focus externally and talked about how to invite diversity into our homes and social circles. But there is one final step. This conversation expands beyond you and your home and me and mine. We are all a part of something bigger—the church. It doesn't matter if you work for a church or not; if you are a follower of Jesus, you have a part to play in it.

In the Bible, the most popular picture of the church is a house. And unfortunately, the *House of God* can easily fall into the same trap we talked about in Part Three, where everyone starts to look, think, and act the same. When people look at our house of worship, what do they see? Do they see a diverse and unified home that welcomes everyone? Or do they see a homogeneous house that doesn't have room for anyone who doesn't fit the mold?

As we've already discussed, Revelation 7:9 paints a picture for where the *House of God* is heading: "After this I looked, and there before me was a great multitude that no one could count, from every nation, tribe, people and language, standing before the throne and before the Lamb."

The end of the story is every tribe, tongue, and nation unified together before God. But we certainly aren't there yet. Our house does not currently look like the picture. We were all supposed to build a house that looks like heaven, but somewhere along the way, we took our eyes off the blueprint. Jesus is the master builder, but these days it feels like we've taken construction into our own hands and drifted a long way away from that goal. Instead of being a house that looks like heaven, we've traded in diversity and unity for division and uniformity.

But there is still hope, and the tide is beginning to turn. The *House of God* can (and should) lead the way in bringing racial healing to the world!

If you are a part of the church in any capacity, you have a part to play, and these final chapters will help you play your role well. We talk about how you can encourage more diversity and open-handed conversations about *God and race* in your community. We then discuss what it means to use both your political and prophetic voices to be a city on a hill during these intense and polarizing times.

It's time for the church to be the church. We are God's plan for the world. And as we strive for diversity in God's House, we'll continue to see transformation in our hearts and households. Let's take up our post and do what God created us to do. It's time for the *House of God* to be a house that looks like heaven.

Take Inventory and Admit the Truth

TAKE AN HONEST LOOK AT YOUR CHURCH

Harsh though it may sound, the facts of history nevertheless bear out this truth: there would be no Black church without racism in the White church.

—JEMAR TISBY

WAYNE FRANCIS

If you were Black and growing up in the South in the eighteenth century, you weren't told only *where* to worship, but you were told *how* to worship. In those days, most slave owners preferred to keep their slaves in the same church building (with segregated seating) to monitor what they were learning. In fact, enslaved people used to have hidden spots, called Hush Harbors, where they could hold services their way. After long days out in the fields, they would sneak off to sing, pray, and connect with God the way they enjoyed. But on Sundays, White folks sat in the front, and Black folks sat in the back (or in the balcony).

One Sunday morning in 1792 a freed slave and passionate Black preacher named Richard Allen walked into a church service at St. George's United Methodist Church in Philadelphia. He entered with his friend Absalom Jones, and the two sat down to pray. What they didn't know is they sat in seats reserved for White people. As they knelt down, a White official yanked Jones to his feet. He protested peacefully, asking whether he could finish his prayer first, but the White man wouldn't let him. Before they knew it, another official was helping to pull Jones up.[1]

From how they treated him, you would've thought he had just robbed a bank, not knelt for prayer. I'm not sure how you train your ushers at your church, but at our church, we take a little different approach.

Allen and Jones stood in disgust and looked around the room as not one single White congregant stood with them to say *that's enough*. So instead, they decided they'd *seen enough*. They turned around and walked out the door. While reflecting on this event, Allen later wrote, "We all went out of the church in a body, and they were no more plagued with us in the church."[2]

That event sparked the beginning of a brand-new church called Bethel African Church. And then from there, Allen went on to found the first historically Black Christian denomination, the African Methodist Episcopal (AME) denomination.[3]

In other words, the Black church started because of racism in the White church.

From there, Sundays continued to be more and more polarizing. The gap between the White and Black churches grew larger and larger through the nineteenth and twentieth centuries, and very few bridges were built (or even attempted) between them. By 1960, Martin Luther King Jr. famously declared, "Eleven o'clock on Sunday morning is one of the most segregated hours, if not the most segregated hours, in Christian America."[4]

Segregation in the church didn't happen by accident. It happened by design. The church is the place where we believe that "there is neither Jew nor Gentile, neither slave nor free, nor is there male and female, for you are all one in Christ Jesus" (Gal. 3:28). You would think we would've led the way in bringing racial healing, but instead of leading, we've lagged.

For centuries, the church has been putting our stamp of approval on things we should've been stomping out. However, the tide is starting to turn. People are beginning to wake up. Thousands have finally decided to stand and say *that's enough*. We have a lot of work to do; we need to make up for some lost time. But to move forward, we first have to go back to our roots, to the very beginning of the church. *Diversity* and *unity* are not the two words we would use to describe the church historically, but those are two words you can use to explain the origin of the church, so let's wind the clocks back to around AD 30.

Beginning in the Beginning

Seven weeks after Jesus's death and resurrection, his followers gathered together in an upper room. With Jesus gone, they had no idea what their next step should be, but the Bible tells us, "they were all with one accord in one place" (Acts 2:1, NKJV). The believers started with unity. They may have had more questions than answers, but one thing they knew for sure was that they needed to be together.

The Jewish Festival of Weeks (Pentecost) was at hand, and "there were staying in Jerusalem God-fearing Jews *from every nation* under heaven" (Acts 2:5, emphasis added). During the Festival of Weeks, Jews from all over the world made a pilgrimage to Jerusalem to celebrate together, which means that people from *every nation* were present.

You see where I'm going, don't you?

The believers were *unified* together and surrounded by a very *diverse* group of people from every nation, and that is the exact moment God decided to launch the church. While they were praying, a mighty rushing wind came through the room, filling all the believers with the Holy Spirit. Crowds heard the sound and came to see what all the commotion was about. There were so many different types of people there that the Holy Spirit had to empower them to speak in languages they could all understand. The origin of the church was so diverse that they literally needed translators. Empowered by the Holy Spirit, the disciples stood up and preached the gospel, and three thousand people were added to the movement that day (Acts 2:41).

I've been a part of a lot of really amazing nights of ministry, but I've never seen anything like that.

By the end of Acts 2, we get a snapshot into the early days of the church: "And all the believers met together in one place and shared everything they had" (Acts 2:44, NLT). People from different tribes and tongues came together, unified by the cross, and shared everything they had with each other.

But somewhere along the way, things changed. We traded

in unity for uniformity and diversity for division. We got caught up in our tribes and forgot that the cross is the thing that brings us together. In Chapter 8, we discussed the danger of the home being homogeneous, but the same is true for the church. People gravitated toward the other people who looked like them, and soon congregations all looked, dressed, and talked the same.

But that's not the way God intended for it to be. We've taken quite a detour since those early days. The church drifted from unity and diversity to the most segregated hour of the week. Ask anyone who is not a believer what their perception of the church is; odds are they will say division way before they say diversity.

We took a detour, but that doesn't mean we are doomed to stay that way. As Paul reminds us, "God . . . gave us the ministry of reconciliation" (2 Cor. 5:18). It's time for the church to step up to the plate and be ministers of reconciliation.

It's time for the church to start stomping out sin instead of stamping it with our approval.

It's time for the church to stop lagging and start leading.

And the only way to move forward is to do one really uncomfortable thing: **take inventory and admit the truth.**

Take Inventory

We want to help you take an honest look at the church you are a part of. Whether you are a church leader or a congregant, we want to equip you with a few steps to take and questions to ask that will shed some light on how your church is doing.

Guilt is not the goal. We know inviting diversity into the church is a long and difficult process—but you have to start somewhere. Over the years, we've realized that in order to move forward toward building a diverse church—a house that looks like heaven—you first have to be honest about where you are. John and I don't have all the answers, but along the way, we have discovered a few helpful places to start. The first three steps are for church leaders, and the last three questions are for anyone who is a part of a church in any capacity.

Let's get started.

Step #1: Look at Your Demographics

It is not an easy time to be a church leader. I mean, let's be real, it's never an easy time to be a church leader, but these days we are faced with more challenges than ever. I get texts from pastors every week who are overwhelmed by the current racial culture and have no idea how to lead during this time. But that doesn't mean you are off the hook. Challenging times are an opportunity to take your leadership to the next level. It's time to get creative.

But if you want to get where you want to go, you first have to know where you are. If John came to visit me in New York and got lost one day, the first thing I would do when he called would be to ask him where he currently is. Because it doesn't matter where he is trying to get; if I don't know where he is, we won't make any progress.

The same is true for your church's journey toward diversity. You have to take a good honest look at where you currently are. What are the racial demographics of your church?

I'm shocked by how many pastors don't know the answer to

that question. Trust me, even if the results aren't pretty, you'll feel better once you know where you are. Even if that pie chart is 99 percent one color and only 1 percent another, at least you'll have a starting point.

The next question to ask is, What are the racial demographics of your city?

Let me take some pressure off you: the goal is not to create a perfectly diverse church. You don't need those slices of the pie chart to all be perfectly equal; that would be nearly impossible in some cities. The game is to try to match the demographics of your church with those of your city.

Go walk around your local Walmart or Target (pronounced Tar-zhay if you are really sophisticated). Look around and take note of the people you see. Does your church look like that? Admitting the truth can be a tough pill to swallow, but once you finally do, you'll be able to move forward. Does your church reflect your city? If not, you know what your new goal is.

Step #2: Look at Your Brand

Once you know how you need to improve in terms of demographics, the next question is to get honest about the message your church is sending to the world. What are you communicating through your church's website and social media accounts? What are people seeing? Based on the pictures and the messaging, would members of a minority demographic feel seen and heard at your church? Or would they feel like they will have to go start their own hush harbor to connect with God the way they prefer?

When two-year-olds don't want to be found, they throw a blanket over their eyes. In their young minds, they believe if they can't see you, you can't see them. Eventually, as we get older, we discover how ludicrous that strategy is. Covering our eyes doesn't mean no one else can see us; it just means we can't see what is all around us.

But I talk to church leaders all the time who are applying the same tactic. Instead of looking at the problem, they cover their eyes, hoping nobody else notices how homogeneous their staff and congregation are. But trust me: they know. Stop looking the other way and calling it leadership. It's time to be mindful of the message we are sending the world. If the only way you can show diversity in your church right now is by using stock photos, that's okay, but now you know what your goal should be.

But let's take this a step further because if the only photos you have of people of color are of them serving or being served and not of them in leadership positions, you've got even more work to do. Again, don't let that discourage you. Let it motivate you to make your church even better than it already is!

Step #3: Look at Your Leadership

I was scrolling through the staff page of a large church the other day, and I noticed that the only people of color on staff were at the bottom under the Facilities and Management Department. That didn't sit well with me. I know the pastor, and that's not his heart. He is working hard to change things, but he has a long journey ahead.

Diversity starts from the top. We are seeing a promising trend in the amount of racial diversity present on the stage in many places. But in several churches, leadership continues to be homogeneous. The goal is not just to present a *picture* of diversity; the goal is to *be* diverse. For lots of churches, the diverse photos on their website aren't an accurate picture of their daily operations and decision making. They have diversity in theory but not in practice.

Good leaders never ask anyone to do something they aren't willing to do themselves. If you are a church leader who is serious about racial healing, you have to take a good, hard look at your leadership team. Are there people around you, at the highest levels, who don't look like you? If you are going to ask your church members to seek diversity in their relationships, make sure you are doing the same.

Of course, you can't (and shouldn't) change this one overnight, but play the long game by being mindful of who you are hiring and who is around you.

Question #1: Am I Willing to Stay?

If you aren't a church leader, you may feel like you have no role to play in your church. But nothing could be further from the truth. You are the church; you have a part to play. What do you do if your church just doesn't get it? Maybe you feel like that church down the street understands this vision for racial healing, and it's tempting you to jump ship.

I know it's tempting to leave and run for greener pastures, but my challenge is this: *Are you willing to stay?* There is more than enough reshuffling going on in the church right now. We don't need more. Instead of running for greener pastures (which is almost always an illusion), what would it look like to stay where you are and bloom where you are planted?

The months after George Floyd's death were incredibly difficult for many Black Christians who were part of predominantly White churches. People were calling and texting me every day, looking for wisdom. They'd watch the White people they serve with respond poorly, and it would make them want to hit the eject button and go back to an all-Black church. Trust me, I know that temptation. When I see a homogeneous *House of God*, I understand the comfort, and I know how it came to that. But I am convinced that fighting to come together and form diverse churches is worth every last ounce of the struggle.

One massive part of taking inventory and admitting the truth is honestly exploring this question: *Am I willing to stay?*

Question #2: What Is a Solution to This Problem?

Here's a little insight that will help you talk to your pastors. They think about the church more than you do. They know where the church is falling short, and they have more than enough people criticizing them and telling them where they are getting it wrong.

If you are serious about creating more diversity in your church, bring solutions to the table instead of problems. Creating is more helpful than critiquing. Instead of just presenting the problem, think about some useful solutions YOU are willing to work on.

Every pastor's dream is to see their people take the initiative and live out the church's mission. You don't need permission from your pastor to have a racially diverse dinner in your own home. Are you working to build the type of church you want? Or are you just critiquing from the sideline? Start focusing on helpful solutions instead of problems.

Question #3: Is Church the Most Diverse Hour of My Week?

Martin Luther King Jr. called Sunday morning the most *segregated* hour of the week. But for those of you who are a part of a diverse church, here's the next challenge. Is Sunday morning actually the most *diverse* hour of your week?

If you serve at a multiethnic church, you learn and grow so much simply because of the people around you. However, are you letting that experience change the way you approach the rest of your week? Attending a diverse church isn't just about checking a box; it's about becoming the type of person who seeks diversity in everyday life. Attending a diverse church is a significant first step, but don't stop there. Be the type of person who is seeking diversity in their social circles all throughout the week!

Take inventory of the other parts of your life. Is church the most diverse hour of your week? If so, what is one step you can take this week to push yourself forward in other areas of your life?

Clear Your Hands

How did that exercise go for you?

Some of you may be really encouraged by what you discovered when you took your inventory. Others are probably feeling a bit discouraged. If the inventory revealed that you have even further to go than you initially thought, I always find it helpful to take a deep breath and remember to start at "one."

Don't feel like you have to change everything overnight. Just start with the people God has placed right in front of you. You may not be where you want to be, and the church you are a part of may have a long, uphill battle ahead of it, but the next person you meet who doesn't look like you is a perfect place to begin.

That's what those ushers at St. George's failed to do. I often sit back and wonder why they yanked Jones to his feet during his prayer on that fateful Sunday. It seems to me that while Jones was bowing down to the God of creation, those ushers were bowing down to the god of segregation. We all bow to the altars of our comforts at times. Jones wanted to talk to God, but church officials felt that the more immediate danger was two Black people who were not seated in the back of the church. In their minds, segregation was more important than experiencing God.

In the next chapter, John asks the question, Who is your king? But the question we need to ask at this moment is, *Where were all the other White congregants?* We don't know how many White people were there that day, but we do know that no one came to stand up to the two who were pulling Jones to his feet. No one stood up and said *that's enough*. Segregation is the fruit of passivism.

Where was the church?

The White church closed its fists and held on to its deeply rooted belief that it was superior. Allen later wrote, "If you love your children, if you love your country, if you love the God of love, clear your hands from slaves, burden not your children or country with them."[5]

Two centuries ago, Richard Allen had the same message we have today: clear your hands of anything that resembles hierarchy based on skin color. We are all one, united under something much more significant: the cross. Don't bow down to the god of segregation; bow down to the creator of the universe. We are one body, and we are in this together. When one part of the body is hurting, we are all hurting, which means when you see people treating someone unjustly because of the color of their skin, stand up and say *that's enough*.

One of the lessons I share with our leadership team is called "Employees Must Wash Their Hands." The talk is designed to remind our team how important their attitude and heart posture toward people are. We've all seen that sign in bathrooms. The sign lets patrons off the hook, but not employees. In the same way, if you are a part of our church, either as a staff member or a volunteer, we hold you to a higher standard. You represent the *House of God*, so keep your hands clear and clean. Our culture is obsessed with Purell for the sake of health; let's be obsessed with purity for the sake of harmony.

The only way to clean your hands is to open them and let go of any old system of oppression you've held on to. Let the old ways fall to the floor and get ready to receive what God has for you next.

Azusa Street

In 1906, William Joseph Seymour, an African American preacher and son of freed slaves, began holding Bible studies in homes in Los Angeles. The meetings started attracting a vast and diverse crowd. People of different ethnicities and socioeconomic statuses began to flock to hear Seymour preach.

Soon homes were so crowded no one could even step foot inside. Seymour soon realized it was time for a bigger space.

He set up shop in an old building on Azusa Street in downtown Los Angeles, and the movement exploded. Before they knew it, a revival was breaking out. There were reports of all types of healing, people being filled with the Holy Spirit, and people giving their lives to Christ.

But one of the most beautiful parts about the revival was the diversity. Daniel Walker called the revival a "multiracial religious event where the color line was washed away in the blood of Jesus."[6] Remember, this was the early twentieth century. The country was still very segregated, and few people were making attempts to come together. But when they caught a glimpse of God's power, people of all races and ethnicities flocked to Azusa Street and worshiped together.

The events at Azusa Street were marked not only by spontaneity and healing but also by diversity and the breaking down of social structure. Black, White, rich, and poor gathered together, united under the cross, to worship and experience freedom. In his article "Visions of Glory," Joe Creech wrote, "Azusa's leaders were ethical restorationists; they abandoned the conventional means by which society ordered reality (education, social status, race, and gender categories); in doing so, they assaulted the status quo."[7]

You can't help but see similarities between Pentecost and Azusa Street. There are no secret formulas for movements of God, but there seem to be common patterns: *unity* and *diversity* seem to set the stage for God to break in and change lives. It's almost like God loves it when his children come together in love and work as one body. God tends to pick diverse spaces to do the most profound work. The Spirit seems to enjoy speaking through unity. Diverse and unified groups can become bill-boards for an onlooking world. A picture of heaven.

Movements of God have happened before, and they will happen again. The question is, Will we get to be a part of it? Passivism will produce only more segregation. It's time for the church to start stomping out the sin we've been stamping with our approval.

And it starts with you. Take an honest look at the role you play in your local church. Are you helping the church move forward toward diversity? If not, it's time to take your first step because it's going to take all of us coming together, unified under a vision of building a house that looks like heaven.

May another person of color never feel like their prayer will be interrupted by the hand of a person who is unwilling to see them as a brother. May we move toward unity, not uniformity. May we continue to embrace different worship and preaching styles. May the church continue to celebrate liturgical and de-monstrative styles, whooping preaching and exegetical preach-ing. And some whooping preaching that is exegetical. May the future be about fusion. And may we all open our hands, jump in, and be a part of the change.

Follow a King, Not a Politician

APPROACHING POLITICS AS A CHRISTIAN

We are so locked into our political identities that there is virtually no candidate, no information, no condition, that can force us to change our minds.

—EZRA KLEIN

JOHN SIEBELING

A few years ago, Leslie and I had an opportunity to travel back to Kenya with our two kids, who were teenagers at the time. It was going to be the first time all four of us were there together, and we couldn't wait to show our kids where we had lived and all the places they grew up hearing stories about.

But as the plane descended into the Nairobi airport, I realized I had spaced out getting us travel visas. Rookie mistake. You can't get into Kenya without visas, so as we got off the plane and stood in the long immigration line, I was praying hard under my breath that the law had changed. When we got to the front of the line, I handed the man our four passports and smiled, probably looking more suspicious than anything. But sure enough, my hopes were dashed as he flipped through the pages and noticed we didn't have visas.

"No problem," the man said kindly. "I just need four fifty-dollar bills."

Do you remember those? Who carries four fifty-dollar bills with them?

As my kids watched, doubting that Leslie and I had really been missionaries for all those years, I had to admit that I didn't have four fifty-dollar bills lying around. Fortunately, they had an ATM in the airport for people like me. Unfortunately, when I walked up to the machine, a big sign on it said *OUT OF ORDER*.

Around that time, I started getting nervous. By the way, it was midnight. Nairobi is a wild place during the day, let alone the middle of the night. Desperate for a solution, I caught the attention of an airport employee and explained my predicament.

"Come," he said in his deep accent, and he took off down a long, dark hallway. I wasn't sure if that was a good sign or a bad sign, but it was the only sign I had, so I took it. We wound through the back hallways and ended up exiting the airport (which I'm sure is highly illegal before passing through immigration) and wove our way through the crowds outside.

Finally, we got to another ATM, and I breathed a sigh of relief. But guess what this one said? *OUT OF ORDER*.

That's about the time I panicked. But at this point, my new friend was just as determined as I was. So while my family sat back in immigration, wondering whether I was still alive, he took me to one final ATM, and it worked! The moral of the story is: *if you take your family to Kenya, get visas beforehand.*

Why would I start a chapter about politics with a story about out-of-order ATMs in Nairobi? Because the order matters.

"Out of order" is sort of an odd phrase, isn't it? Why don't we just say "broken"? Because we all intuitively understand that when something inside a machine is firing out of order, the entire system breaks down.

The same is true for you and me. God created us in his image, and we function best when we function according to his design. The Bible says God is a God of order (1 Cor. 14:33), and when we follow that order, we operate at our highest potential.

However, when we get our priorities out of order, things fall apart because *the order matters.*

With that in mind, I have a big announcement to make. This announcement may surprise a few people, it may anger a few people, and it may catch a few people off guard. Are you ready?

Here goes: *God is not a Republican.*

Okay, I've got another one I have to make. This one may be just as shocking or frustrating to others of you: *God is not a Democrat.*

Have I managed to offend everyone yet? Just in case I haven't, let me try one final announcement: *God is not an American.*

I'll stop now, but the thing is, I'm a pastor. I love the church, I've given my life to help build the church, and I can't help but notice a trend that worries me. We've gotten some priorities *out of order.* As Jesus followers, we are children of God and citizens of heaven. That is our identity. However, I see a rising number of Christians who seem to identify with their political party before their God. Sadly, there is a wave of Christians who know more about who is running in the primaries than they know about how to make God's Kingdom primary. It's not that this knowledge is wrong; it's just *out of order.* What identifies a follower of Jesus is *who* and *what* that person seeks first. Jesus said it's when we seek *first* his Kingdom that all other things will be *added* to us; maybe our lack of seeking in this way is what has kept us *divided.*

I know I'm treading in dangerous water here, but in scripture, anytime someone makes a god out of anything else (a statue, a person, or a golden calf), it doesn't go well. When God gave Moses the Ten Commandments, he started with "You shall have no other gods before me" (Exod. 20:3).

Have you made a god out of your political party? There is a difference between being a Jesus follower who happens to vote Republican and being a Republican who happens to follow Jesus. And there is a difference between being a Jesus follower who happens to vote Democrat and being a Democrat who happens to follow Jesus.

The order matters.

When our identity is in our political party instead of our devotion to Jesus, we will start fitting God into our political box.

Politics are a significant part of our lives, but they are not the ultimate thing. I'm not deliberately trying to get underneath your skin, but you need to know that you can be a Christian and vote Democrat *or* Republican. The church does not exist for either political party; the church exists to glorify God. The church is not the place where we fly the Democratic or Republican flag. It is the place where we raise a white flag of surrender to God and declare we are first and foremost citizens of heaven.

I love how D. A. Carson put it in his book *Love in Hard Places*:

> *The church is . . . made up of natural enemies. What binds us together is not common education, common race, common income levels, common politics, common nationality, common accents, common jobs, or anything else of that sort. Christians come together . . . because they have all been saved by Jesus Christ and owe him a common allegiance. . . . They are a band of natural enemies who love one another for Jesus' sake.*[1]

A Picture of Heaven

In the last chapter, Wayne reminded us of how the church began. We were a diverse group of people, unified by the gospel. But that's not just how we *started*; it's how we will *end*. Remember, as we've been talking about, Revelation 7:9 paints a picture of where we are heading, and it's a picture of a diverse group of people all worshiping God together.

Black and *White* worshiping together.

Rich and *poor* worshiping together.

Democrat and *Republican* worshiping together.

A diverse group unified by the beauty of God.

Today, we find ourselves somewhere in between those two moments. We are on a journey toward unity and diversity, but we've taken quite a detour. Along the way, there have been times when we've gotten off course. Letting our identities get caught up in our political parties is a good example. Unfortunately, when we decided to bow at our political party's feet instead of to our God, we traded in unity for polarized political opinions. We need to talk about politics because political identity is one of the major things keeping the church from coming together.

And this political polarization has significant racial implications.

We have to take a step back and make sure we have the order correct. Should the church be on the left or the right? Wrong question. The government sits on the shoulders of Jesus (Isa. 9:6). Which means he alone bears the strength to balance both sides. The much better question is, How can we be a house that looks like heaven?

The challenging part about that question is we aren't in heaven yet, are we? On earth, we need rules and regulations, which means we need leaders and elections. In short, we need politics. Our job is to learn how to engage in politics without forgetting who's King. Fortunately, Jesus stepped out of heaven and entered into this world to do just that—show us how to engage in politics without losing the order. So let's address the elephant in the room (or is it a donkey?) and talk about how Jesus handled political questions.

Who Is Your King?

On one of the final days leading up to Jesus's arrest and crucifixion, he was walking through the temple courts when the Pharisees cornered him and asked him a polarizing question.

They asked, "Is it right to pay the imperial tax to Caesar or not?" (Matt. 22:17).

That was a trap. Remember, the Jews weren't free in the first century. Rome ruled the world, and they did so by having an extensive military. Where did they get money to pay all those soldiers' salaries? By taxing the very people they were oppressing. Imagine being a hard-working Jew in the first century and having to work twice as hard to put food on the table because you are paying taxes to fund your oppressors.

And then one day you hear the religious leaders ask Jesus whether it's right to pay taxes to Caesar. If he said yes, he would sound like another puppet on a string doing what Rome told him. But if he said no, the soldiers would haul him off immediately. The world was trying to force Jesus to use his political voice at the expense of his prophetic voice.

Jesus saw the trap from a mile away. Instead of answering their question, he posed a new one. He told them to show him a denarius (the coin used to pay the tax), and then he asked whose image was on the coin.

"Caesar's," they replied. Then he said to them, "So give back to Caesar what is Caesar's, and to God what is God's" (Matt. 22:21).

That is one of those mic drop moments in the Bible (Jesus had several of them throughout his ministry). The weight of what he said gets a little lost on us today, but everyone present in the temple knew exactly what he said.

"Whose image is on a coin?" is a callback to the first page of the Bible where God creates humans in his image (Gen. 1:26–27). Caesar's face is on the coin, great. Give him what he's asking for, no big deal. But more important, whose image is on you? The much more significant invitation is to give to God what is God's. Since God made you in his image, the message is to lay down your entire life to God.

Jesus challenged why the Pharisees would ask him a question about taxes when there is a much bigger story at hand. He was checking their order. Did they believe they were children of God who happened to live in a world where they had to pay taxes to Caesar, or had they made Caesar their god?

In other words, he was asking the question, *Who is your King?*

It's a big question. Too many of us are submitting to a king who has to be voted in instead of one who needs to be surrendered to. Jesus didn't shrink back from using his political voice. Instead, he utilized it to bolster his prophetic voice. The Pharisees wanted Jesus to give them a political answer, but he gave them a prophetic one. He willingly walked into the trap and then used it to help everyone check their hearts. Was God still their King, or was Rome?

The story of the Bible is much bigger than that of our nation, and it's much bigger than your political party. It's a story about the creator of the universe inviting us to come together, unified by the cross, to worship as one.

Have you lost sight of that bigger story? These days it's easy to do. Watch enough news reports or scroll through enough political posts on social media, and before long, you'll find yourself putting politicians on the throne. Do you see why the order matters?

We can engage in politics, but we need to be followers of Jesus.

Get in the habit of asking yourself this question: *Is Jesus really my King?* It's a sobering and grounding question that brings us back to the bigger story. When we are honest enough to admit that politics can, at times, sneak by and take the throne, we have an opportunity to stop, repent, and get back to following Jesus instead of a politician.

Where Is Our Edge?

The fastest way for the church to lose its edge is for it to get its priorities out of order. Anytime a church starts following a politician instead of the King, it begins to forfeit its power to tell a much bigger and more beautiful story to a world that is longing to hear it.

What's the first thing that pops into your head when you hear the word *prophetic*? For some, especially those with a charismatic background, you may be picturing some guy on a stage saying, "Thus saith the Lord." But prophetic does not just mean foretelling; when I use the word *prophetic*, I am referring to an ability to speak God's word into a situation. I mean having enough of an edge about you to let God use you to cut into culture like a double-edged sword and speak truth to a world that desperately needs it.

The church is God's plan for the earth. We are here to be a city on a hill, a light shining bright into a dark world. We can get so caught up trying to have a political voice that we lose our prophetic one. When we lose our prophetic voice, we lose our edge; like a dull knife, we become more of a decoration than a useful tool. If the *House of God* is going to lead the way in reconciliation, we need to find our edge again; we need to recapture our prophetic voice.

When the church is at its best, it really can change things. Spiritual leaders spearheaded most of the significant movements in the history of the world. When we remember Dr. Martin Luther King Jr., we think of him as a political leader. What we forget is that Dr. King was a pastor before anything else. He loved the church enough to call it out. He once warned, "If the church does not recapture its prophetic zeal, it will become an irrelevant social club without moral or spiritual authority."[2]

Swords or Social Clubs?

When the church loses its edge, it loses its ability to carve out the path of reconciliation and starts drifting toward the path of least resistance. We stop being a picture of heaven and become a picture of the culture. We trade in our swords for a seat at our social club. In The Color of Compromise, Jemar Tisby made a fascinating historical observation: "Many white Christians comforted themselves with the myth that slavery allowed them to more adequately care for the material and spiritual needs of enslaved Africans."[3]

Just a few centuries ago, the church was full of White slave owners. On Sundays, slave owners sang songs and read about Jesus's call to love their neighbors, and then they went home and forced their neighbors into lives of slavery. No condemnation, no callouts from their Life Group, no church discipline—everyone just looked the other way and went right along living their lives.

How could it get to that point?

We've come a long way since then, but the same principle

applies today. Humans have a dangerous ability to justify each other's behaviors and actions. When we lose our edge, we stop blazing a new way forward and drift back to what Dr. King called an irrelevant social club, more concerned with fitting in than standing out.

Prophetic Zeal

Jesus had an edge to him. He never let injustice fly. Yes, he is the compassionate, loving shepherd we love. But as we've talked about throughout this book, he also wasn't afraid to stand up and use his voice. When people encountered Jesus, they were challenged and changed; some went away angry, some went away sad, but no one left feeling indifferent.

If we lose our passion and our edge, we are in danger of becoming just another voice that conveniently fits whatever mold culture has presented us. We can't lean in to convenience and comfort at the expense of our convictions.

Have we split the body left and right?

Jesus came into a polarized world and brought people together. Recently, Wayne shared a blog post with me from his friend Scott Sauls that encapsulates this point well:

Jesus brought Simon, an anti-government Zealot, and Matthew, a government employee, into his group of disciples. Of the four Gospel writers, Matthew alone points out this fact, signaling that loyalties to Jesus transcend all other loyalties, including political ones. Even Simon and Matthew, two people on polar

*opposite political extremes, were able to live and love in commu-
nity together. Why? Because instead of creating dividing walls,
Jesus breaks down dividing walls.[4]*

It didn't matter which side of the political fence you were
on; when you heard Jesus speak and watched how he lived,
you wanted to follow him. As his followers, we need to recapture that spirit. Are you putting up walls or tearing them
down?

If we want to tear down walls, we need our edge back, we
need to recapture our prophetic zeal and use our prophetic
voice. It's time to remember that the church is God's Plan A
for the world. It's time to use our voices to announce the good
news that God wants his church to be a unified people.

Yes, we have a political duty. But there is a way to use your
political voice without hindering your prophetic one. Instead
of letting our politics steal our power, let's use the conversation to point people toward Jesus. As the old adage goes, *Be in
the world, but not of it.*

Remember, our goal is to engage in politics but follow Jesus.
To do that effectively, let's get practical and talk about how we
can use both our political and prophetic voices.

Political Voice

Politics are a powerful way to bring change in the world. The
question is, How should Christians fulfill their political duty?

The first-century followers of Jesus had very little to say

about politics. You can sum up their message with one word: *honor.* To honor means to respect and give dignity to a person. Honor doesn't mean you have to like someone, but it does mean you need to show that person respect. The Bible instructs us to "show respect for all people [treat them honorably], love the brotherhood [of believers], fear God, honor the king" (1 Pet. 2:17, AMP). Peter didn't say "cancel all people"; he said the opposite. Show them respect. The truth is, every political leader you disagree with is created in the image of God. That doesn't mean you have to agree with them; it means you are called to honor them.

At our church one of our values is that we honor all people. We honor up, we honor down, we honor all the way around. Honor, like love, has no exemptions.

To truly grasp how strong Peter's words are, we need a little context. Some translations say "honor the emperor," which means Peter was talking about a man named Nero. He was an awful man who hated Christians. The city of Rome burned to the ground in AD 64, and Emperor Nero blamed the Christians for starting the fire. He used a horrific event as a way to condemn Christians. Suddenly, anyone who continued to profess Christ became a marked man or woman. Christians were crucified, beheaded, set on fire, and mauled to death by lions in the coliseum. In the first century, persecution wasn't being asked to wear a mask during a pandemic; it was being torn apart by wild animals.

And Peter told the church to *honor* the man calling the shots.

If you are a follower of Jesus, you don't have to like your leaders, you don't have to agree with them, and you don't have to keep your mouth shut. But you are called to honor them.

And yes, that verse is just as true when that *other party* is in the Oval Office.

We aren't the first group of people to experience political polarization. It's always been that way. Britain's election in 1774 was particularly brutal. It was marked by hate, violence, and bribery. John Wesley was a prominent religious leader during the election, and one night he made this entry in his journal:

> *I met those of our society who had votes in the ensuing election, and advised them 1. To vote, without fee or reward, for the person they judged most worthy, 2. To speak no evil of the person they voted against, and 3. To take care their spirits were not sharpened against those that voted on the other side.*[5]

Those three steps just about cover it. You have a vote, use it! But seek God's guidance as you check the box. After that, watch what you say about the other candidates, and don't let yourself get bitter or angry at anyone who didn't vote like you.

That doesn't mean we can't speak up against the candidate we disagree with, but let's be honest: there is a way to do that without being evil. Likewise, we can engage in conversations with people who don't vote like us without them ending poorly. Peter says, "Therefore, rid yourselves of all malice and all deceit, hypocrisy, envy, and slander of every kind" (1 Pet. 2:1).

When we get the order right and remember God is our King, we affirm God's image in people regardless of their political party. With that as our baseline, we are freed up to jump in and use our political voice without harming our prophetic duty.

Prophetic Voice

If using your prophetic voice overwhelms you, remember, by *prophetic*, we mean reminding the world what God's word has to say.

If we want to do that effectively, we can take a cue from a prophet of old—a man named Micah, who lived in Israel around 700 BC and spent his life warning that destruction was coming. That's not an easy message to deliver, but in chapter 6 of the book of Micah we get some insight into how he learned to give that message:

> *He has told you, O man, what is good;*
> *and what does the Lord require of you*
> *but to do justice, and to love kindness,*
> *and to walk humbly with your God? (Mic. 6:8, ESV)*

We could write a whole other book on that single verse, but let's keep it simple and talk through those three steps.

Do Justice

Justice is a major theme in the Bible. Whether it was children, people with leprosy, Samaritans, or the blind, Jesus was always speaking up for oppressed people and speaking out against the systems that were oppressing them. But he didn't just speak; he also got to work. He put his money where his mouth was. He didn't just encourage; he healed. He didn't just speak life; he brought people back from the dead. He didn't just talk about justice; he acted. So if you want to use your prophetic voice, the first step is to find practical and helpful ways to get to work.

Love Kindness

In Galatians 5, Paul lists kindness as a fruit of the Spirit, a sign you are on the right track. Micah goes as far as to say we need to learn to *love* it. Love is a strong word. He doesn't tell us to tolerate kindness out of obligation; he instructs us to fall in love with kindness. Do you love the people you are trying to influence enough to be kind to them? How about when they persecute you? Anyone can be nice to people who are nice to them, but prophets are rarely popular; are you ready to react to persecution with kindness?

Walk Humbly

Above all, if we want to speak God's truth into our culture, we must be humble. If you want people to listen to what you have to say, don't speak down to them—walk over to them. That's the example of Jesus. In humility, he stepped out of heaven and came to us, taking the form of a lowly man, whom we now exalt.

If you are struggling to find humility, start by praying for the people who bother you. Paul tells Timothy, "I urge, then, first of all, that petitions, prayers, intercession and thanksgiving be made for all people—for kings and all those in authority, that we may live peaceful and quiet lives in all godliness and holiness" (1 Tim. 2:1–2).

When was the last time you prayed for the political leader you have a problem with? When was the last time you prayed for that person you always argue politics with?

The authority to prophetically speak into their lives comes from having the humility to pray for the people who persecute us.

Stay Salty

Right before he ascended into heaven, Jesus's followers asked him, "Lord, are you at this time going to restore the kingdom to Israel?" (Acts 1:6). They still didn't get it. They were still playing the wrong game.

From the beginning, we have been searching for political answers to spiritual problems.

If you are a Christian, Jesus is your King, and Jesus is the answer. Yes, we are here on this earth, so yes, we honor our leaders and speak up for what we believe. But at the end of the day, our citizenship is in heaven. As you participate in politics, do not forget that your identity is a follower of Jesus and a child of God.

Jesus called us the "salt of the earth" (Matt. 5:13); we are here to preserve and add flavor to this place. We are called to be salt, but somewhere along the way, we lost our saltiness.

In the eighteenth century, when the White church forced Black people out the door, resulting in Black people starting their own denomination, we lost our saltiness.

In the nineteenth century, when White slave owners sat around the table, secure in their belief that what they were doing was noble, we lost our saltiness.

In the twentieth century, when slavery was abolished, but the church remained segregated, we lost our saltiness.

And today, when we identify our political party as God's political party, we lose our saltiness.

The church needs to get its saltiness back. I don't want historians to remember our era of the church as the time politics kept us segregated. I want us to be remembered as the era of the church that built bridges instead of barriers and brought a polarized country together at the foot of the cross. When someone walks into our church, I want that person to feel comfortable no matter who they are, where they are from, or which party they voted for. And I want that to be true for every congregation, in every part of the nation, every week. We can get there, but first, we need to get our edge back. It's time to rediscover our prophetic voice!

Reorder

When an ATM is out of order, it is no use to anyone. All of the money is still inside, but there is no way to get it out. The machine still has all of its potential, but none of its power.

I can't help but notice the same is true for many Christians. We are image-bearers of the divine, agents of reconciliation, here to make a difference in the world. But when we elevate the importance of a political party above God, we forfeit so much of our power.

Is that true about you?

If people no longer seem interested in engaging in conversations with you, it may be time to reorder.

If people try to change the subject every time you start talking politics, it may be time to reorder.

If you feel like you've been losing some of your authority, it may be time to reorder.

Nobody wants to hear about the love of Jesus from someone who spends the majority of their energy throwing stones at their political enemies. Authority is rooted in the creator, not the culture. It's time to reorder!

That ATM will lie dormant as long as things fire out of order, but as soon as the mechanic comes through and puts things back in the right order, all the potential turns back into power, and a panicked former missionary can get the money he needs to buy a visa.

Once we finally made our way through the airport, the rest of our family trip to Nairobi was incredible. That city shaped Leslie and me in so many profound ways. And there was something special about getting to pass down those stories and experiences to our kids. When I was young, my dad taught me there are moments in life when you need to stand and say *that's enough*. And that's the message I want to pass along, not just to my kids, but to everyone reading this book, because unity is worth fighting for.

It may not always be easy, and it won't always be popular, but when we get the order right, our potential turns back into power. Political cycles will come and go, but with our prophetic voice, we can remind the world that the throne has always and will always belong to the one who reigns forever.

Take the Plunge

STAY COMMITTED TO THE FIGHT

WAYNE FRANCIS

"Brother Francis! Brother Francis!"

I could recognize Jerry's voice anywhere. He's got one of those deep, authoritative, pastoral tones. But I certainly wasn't expecting to hear him as I strolled through a random locker room at a fitness club in Los Angeles. I had just finished a workout and was about to head back to my hotel when I heard him (along with everyone else in the locker room and probably people in New Zealand) yelling my name.

I turned around and saw him sitting in the corner of what looked like a pool, with a huge smile on his face. Jerry, like my friend Jimmy, is a "Big Body Benz" who demands everyone's attention in the room.

"Brother Francis, come on in, the water is fine."

To be honest, I didn't really want to go, and since we were in a locker room surrounded by strangers, I wished he'd stop referring to me with that old school "brother" talk and stick with "Wayne." Plus, it was at the end of a long day and a tough workout, and I just wanted to get back to my hotel. But he wouldn't take no for an answer. Eventually, he wore me down. Thinking it was a normal pool, I walked over and jumped right in.

What I didn't know until that moment was that it wasn't a pool . . . it was a cold plunge.

The water shocked me. My body tensed up and began shivering uncontrollably. I panicked. Between gasps for air, I started reaching for the rails to pull myself out of the water.

"No. No. Stay in it." Jerry's boisterous voice was now pointed and directed straight at me from the other side of the cold plunge. "You're okay, just breathe. Your body will regulate."

My lungs felt like blocks of ice. Everything inside me wanted to bounce out. But I had come this far, so I did my best to stay put. As Jerry cheered me on, I took one deep breath after the next, and my body slowly settled in and acclimated to the water.

Here's the thing about me and cold water: I know myself well enough to know that I never would've gotten in that pool if I had taken my time. I don't even take cold showers in the summertime. If I had dipped my toe in to feel the water first, that would've been all she wrote. I would've grabbed my bag, wished *Brother Jerry* well, and been out of there.

When it comes to the cold plunge, there ain't no half-steppin'. My only shot at success was full and immediate immersion.

That's where I feel many churches are right now when it comes to jumping into the racial healing conversation. When I talk to a lot of pastors, it feels like they want to be a part of the solution, but they don't want to go all the way. So instead, they dip a toe into the water to see how it feels. They do one sermon on unity, and then they pull back and check what it did to their attendance. Then maybe they get in up to their knees, by doing an entire series on racial healing. But then they hop out and quickly open their inbox to make sure they didn't anger anyone. And then, if they are feeling really brave, they slowly start to sink into the cold plunge and create diversity groups for a semester before jumping back out of the water to look at the giving to see if it's gone up or down.

They're half-steppin'.

You've stuck with us this far, so I feel like I can just be honest at this point. Half-steppin' in the fight for racial healing is miserable. The water is way too cold. The shock is too strong. Unless you jump right in and embrace the role, you are going to drive yourself nuts.

Plus, if you don't stay in, you miss out on all the advantages. I have crazy friends who take ice baths every day, and they tell me the only way to experience the benefits is to get all the way in and stay there. And I believe them because, after a few minutes of pain in the cold plunge, I felt a new surge of energy rush through my veins. My senses heightened, and I felt like a whole new man. But if you want to experience the benefits of a cold plunge, you have to resist the urge to jump ship.

It's time for the church to do the same. No more jumping ship after one sermon series on racial reconciliation; put it in your annual teaching rotation. No more mentioning a desire for diversity as an afterthought; make it a core value and revisit it often. Don't just start diversity groups; stick with diversity groups. Multiply them over time. Go all in! One sermon, one group, or one guest speaker will not get us where we need to be.

That's half-steppin'.

And half-steppers don't create houses that look like heaven.

You have to be ALL in to do that!

When we decide to take the plunge and go all in, committing to being agents of racial healing, the water may shock us for a second. We may get some push back, and some people may leave or unfollow us. But if we can just keep breathing through it and commit to the long haul, we will find that new life and fresh energy are waiting for us on the other side. We have to be all in, church!

When you commit with your whole heart, you won't settle for a half-step.

We need to kill our tentativeness and match our talk with our walk. No more tiptoeing. No more half-steppin'!

The Bite That Broke the Camel's Back

The Apostle Paul was a crazy church planter who was always on the move. God used him to do some amazing things, but his life was far from easy; he had his fair share of trials. In 2 Corinthians 11:23–25, he made a list for us that included

* Several trips to prison

* Multiple near-death experiences

* Five whippings (thirty-nine lashes apiece)

* Three beatings (with rods)

* Stoned once (by rocks not weed)

* Three shipwrecks

* And an entire night adrift at sea

That's quite a track record. And can I say, if I've already been in two shipwrecks, I'm not getting back on a boat. But that's who Paul was; he wasn't half-steppin'. The world gave him plenty of reasons to call it quits and jump out of the cold plunge, but he was a man on a mission.

The tale of one of those shipwrecks is in Acts 27. While he and his companions were sailing to Italy (if you are picturing that Mediterranean cruise you went on a few summers ago, you couldn't be more wrong), they ran into a giant storm at sea. Remember, there were no iPhones or weather apps at this point; they just got blindsided. They fought the wind and the rain for fourteen days until they finally saw an island called Malta, but when they attempted to get there, the ship got stuck on a sandbar, and the waves tore the boat to pieces, forcing the crew to swim for shore.

If I had been one of the crew who finally made it to the beach, I probably would have wanted to curl up into a ball and cry for a few hours. But instead of throwing a pity party, Paul got straight to work, searching for firewood—because, of course, it was a cold and rainy day. That's how trials work: when it rains, it pours.

The people of Malta made a big fire for the stranded sailors, and as Paul was placing fuel on it (probably pieces of their wrecked boat that had washed ashore), a poisonous snake, driven out by the heat of the fire, lunged out and latched onto his hand.

I'm a church planter who has gone through a lot for the gospel, but snakes are where I draw the line. I hate snakes. I know I'm not supposed to hate. But I hate snakes. There is a reason the Bible likens snakes to the devil. I mean, I do like snakes that have been converted into belts, wallets, purses, and key fobs, but I hate the rest. I know I spoke out against cancel culture earlier, but I'd like to cancel snakes.

The locals were terrified. Apparently, this was no garter snake. This was one of those "see you later" types of snakes. They were convinced that Paul was going to swell up and die. So, for those of you keeping track at home, Paul was just trying to do good. He was trying to bring the gospel to the ends of the earth. But as he went, he got into three shipwrecks, one of which led him to an island, and as he was trying to stay alive, a poisonous snake latched onto his hand.

If I were Paul, at this point, I'd have some words for God. "Lord, I'm trying to do good. I'm not out on a mission to push grandmas down the stairs; I'm planting churches, but people are trying to kill me, ships are crashing into sandbars, and now snakes."

That may have been the bite that broke the camel's back for me. I may have called it quits and retired to Palm Springs to spend the rest of my days frustrated about my golf game instead of being frustrated about the church.

If you've dipped your foot into the cold plunge and started fighting for racial unity, you may know that type of pain all too well. It was the heat of the fire that drove the snake out in the first place, and race is a hot topic that can bring the worst out of people. Hopefully, you haven't been bitten by any snakes, but people's words and criticisms can be just as venomous.

Fighting for unity and diversity in the church is not easy. People don't like change, and they aren't shy about letting you know that.

The pain can be heavy and suffocating, and then on top of that, John and I have the nerve to step in and ask you to open your hands. The words *hopeless, angry,* and *apathetic* seem almost too tame to describe how you may feel.

The pain can make you want to pull out of the cold plunge and go back to your hotel. But the reason I gravitate toward Paul's story is because he didn't give up. He didn't let the poison paralyze him. Instead, the Bible says, he "shook off the snake into the fire and was unharmed" (Acts 28:5, NLT).

What? Shook it off? Unharmed by a poisonous snake bite?

The locals were so impressed that they decided he was a god, and Paul, never one to shy away from an open door, used it as an opportunity to preach the gospel.

The pain was real. His hand was throbbing; he had every right to close his fist and be done. But instead, he opened his hands and turned his pain into a platform.

The question is not *How can we avoid wounds?*

The question is *Can we keep on steppin'?*

How would you answer that question? Can you keep going? Can you stay in the fight? Can you keep your hands open?

If you've ever found it difficult to answer yes to any of those questions, you are in good company. I know the feeling. The rocks of racism are real, and they aren't easy to shake off. But whenever I feel myself starting to half-step, I've always found the rest of this story at the end of the book of Acts to be incredibly helpful.

Bites or Blessings?

Snakes bites were nothing new for the people of Malta. They happened all the time. But what they never saw was someone shake that snake off and keep on walking. It wasn't the bite that impressed them; it was the way Paul responded.

The chief official of the island was a man named Publius. When he heard about Paul's encounter with the snake, he was so impressed that he asked him to pray for his sick father. Paul had just been bitten on the hand by a poisonous snake. He could've staggered off and been done with it all, but instead, he opened his wounded hand and laid it on the sick man, healing him.

Here's what I love: Paul was traveling with a man named Luke (who went on to write the book of Acts), but Luke wasn't just an author, he was a physician. If my dad were sick and my two options for help are a doctor and some crazy church planter who seems to have a knack for shipwrecks, I'm choosing the doctor.

Luke may have had more degrees than a thermometer, but God didn't use the one with the MD to heal; he used the one with the wound. Paul's power was on the other side of his pain. *The hand with the bite became an instrument of healing to others.*

Paul didn't let the poison paralyze him; he didn't clench his fists. Despite the pain, he opened his hands back up, and as a result, "then all the other sick people on the island came and were healed" (Acts 28:9, NLT). That's the power of wounds. They have the ability to reach others just by virtue of how you respond.

What about you? Is the fear of a little persecution keeping you half-steppin'?

What would happen if you extended that wounded hand of yours from a biting remark from someone in your church? What if you didn't allow the venomous wound from that blogger set you back? What if that insensitive joke in a boardroom didn't destroy your self-worth?

But Wayne, are you saying that I should just shake off direct racism? How do I shake off the fact that our prison system is geared to keep generations of Black people incarcerated?

I'm not saying this is easy. If you've been the target of one too many rocks of racism, you may be tempted to take your clenched fists to your grave. Many people have. But persecution is nothing new. The thing that gets people's attention is when we respond to trials with open hands. The people who make history and bring about reconciliation are those who don't let the poison paralyze them. Instead, they shake off the snake and open their hands back up to the world.

That's where healing begins.

What if your bites are a blessing?

Power is almost always forged by pain. I know the pain is real, and I know the anger is justified, but what if the persecution and the trials have actually set you up to be a healing agent in your community? We aren't immune to pain. However, when it comes down to someone who needs healing, it's a wounded hand that brings healing. It's people with wounds, not just people with degrees.

What if the venomous words that made you want to walk away from your church could actually bring about healing? Could your pain end up having a more redemptive purpose that is even larger than you thought? Could it be that there is power on the other side of your pain?

Remind Me Tomorrow

After George Floyd's death, one of my good friends, a White pastor with a predominantly White church, asked me to jump on a Zoom call to talk to his staff about racism. I made my coffee, sat in my chair, and hit the link he sent me. But as the Zoom call opened up, I couldn't see anyone; I could only hear them. The screen was black.

This was right around the time we were all learning what Zoom was. You remember those days—when the world shut down, and Zoom's stock prices shot up. I was still a Zoom newbie at the time and honestly had no idea how to troubleshoot this problem.

I couldn't see them.

They couldn't see me.

"Wayne, is your video on? Click 'join with video.'"

"Is there something blocking your camera?"

"Try closing the meeting and getting back in."

"Let me send you a new link."

Some of you are getting anxious just reading this. We were all on a tight schedule, but nothing was working. And since we couldn't see each other, we were talking over each other, stumbling over words, and running out of precious meeting time.

Something wasn't right. There was a bug in the system.

And then a little message popped up telling me I needed an update. The truth is, my computer had been telling me that for a long time. You know what I'm talking about, don't you? How great is the *Remind me tomorrow* button? It's the best excuse in the book. It allows us to keep putting it off and putting it off. Unfortunately, I had told my computer to *Remind me tomorrow* one too many times, and now I couldn't see the people on the other side of the screen.

That's a great picture of what we are currently experiencing in the church. For years, pain and conflict have existed just beneath the surface, but we kept pushing it off. Whenever there were little warning signs, we'd all agree to click that *Remind me tomorrow* button and continue on with our lives. Facing the pain would be more shocking to our system than jumping into a cold plunge. The problem is that we put it off for so many years, eventually we stopped being able to see each other.

Once I realized that I needed an upgrade, we stopped bickering back and forth. I installed it, restarted my computer, jumped back on Zoom, and sure enough, I could see all their faces. With the time we had left, we had a great conversation about *God and race*, where we could actually look one another in the eye.

Have you stopped being able to see the people on the other side of the race conversation? Maybe you can still hear their voices or see their posts, but if you are honest, is there so much distance between you and them that you can't even see them? Maybe you find yourself saying things like

I will never be able to understand how you could believe _____.

I don't get how anyone could possibly vote for _____.

Why would you ever listen to _____?

We need an upgrade. When we stop procrastinating and let God do the work in our lives that we know he wants to do, we'll feel better afterward. God will go in and get rid of some pesky bugs that have made themselves at home in our hearts and in the church. Then suddenly, we'll realize we can actually see the people on the other side of the conversation. Even if we disagree with them, we'll be able to understand their perspective and empathize with their pain.

After Rodney King was beaten in 1991, we clicked *Remind me tomorrow*. After the OJ Simpson trial in 1995, the case of the century that revealed how split our nation was on racial issues on a major scale, we clicked *Remind me tomorrow*. After the deaths of Amadou Diallo (1999), Eric Garner (2014), and Ahmaud Arbery (2020), we kept clicking *Remind me tomorrow*, until the firmware in our communities and the operating system of our culture crashed.

Today is the day the Lord has made; don't push *Remind me tomorrow*. Install the update. And no, I'm not still talking about your computer (although practically speaking, you really should install that update). I'm talking about the church stepping up to the plate and acknowledging what has always been true, but has never been popular. The truth is, the church has caused a lot of pain over the years, and we've ignored it for too long. It's time to face it, acknowledge it, and let the healing process begin.

We are called to be agents of healing. Stop clicking *Remind me tomorrow*. Stop putting off till tomorrow what should be done today. Stop tiptoeing into the shallow end. No more half-steppin'! The water may be cold, it may shock your system at first, but it's time to take the plunge.

Are You Half-Steppin'?

How do you know if you are half-steppin'? Here are a few questions to ask yourself.

Are you a part of a local church? The truth is, you can't build something you aren't willing to invest in. If we want to see the *House of God* become a place of unity and diversity, we need to be dedicated to it. If you want to have a real voice, don't settle for being a ventriloquist. We keep throwing our voices to other sources instead of speaking up right where we are. Actions speak louder than words. You don't get a voice just by attending a few services every once in a while, when convenient. You get a voice by jumping in and getting involved.

Do you serve on a team? Teams are the best way to connect with people who are not like you. They are the best place to not only use your gifts and talents, but also find healing.

Do you pray for your pastor? Your pastor needs divine wisdom to lead well during a challenging time in our country. Your prayers are critical.

Do you contribute financially? If you do, it will make a difference in how your church impacts underserved people—particularly those marginalized because of the color of their skin.

After pastoring for nearly twelve years, I see people half-step in these areas way too often, not realizing God will do something big with our full steps, even if they seem like small steps. Just jump in, and you'll realize the water is fine.

Don't Grow Weary

Are you ready to go all in? Are you ready to play your part in bringing racial healing to this world? You've made it this far, so I'm going to assume the answer is yes. Here's the last thing I'll say: *Don't grow weary.*

When conversations about racial healing don't go your way, you'll be tempted to throw in the towel.

When you realize being the change you want to see in the church is going to cost you something, you'll think about giving up.

When people turn their backs on you for speaking up, a part of you will want to just shut your mouth and play it safe.

In short: half-steppin' is tempting.

I get it. The road to racial healing is a long, winding one full of detours and roadblocks. It feels like it's uphill the whole way. You may find yourself getting tired along the way—I know I certainly do.

But we can't let a little fatigue slow us down!

We have to keep fighting to open our hands.

Paul never let snakes, stones, or shipwrecks slow him down. He earned the right to write, "Let us not become weary in doing good, for at the proper time we will reap a harvest if we do not give up" (Gal. 6:9). Paul had every excuse to give up and give in, but he kept going. He kept pressing in. He understood that to reap a harvest, he had to persevere through the trials and the storms and make it to the finish line.

I hope people say the same thing about me one day, and as you approach the end of this book, I know you have the same goal for your life, and you can do it. You just have to be willing to dive in, take the plunge, and keep on breathing.

Regardless of where you land, I can't let you tiptoe away from this issue. We've been ballet dancers pirouetting around this topic for too long.

Jerry wouldn't let me tiptoe into the cold plunge that day in the fitness center, and I'm healthier for it. My sister wouldn't let me tiptoe through the mailroom because of my salary, and I'm stronger for it. My father refused to let me tiptoe through a comfortable and homogeneous upbringing, and I grew so much for it. John continues to encourage me to keep fighting for a diverse church, and I'm a better pastor for it.

And of course, the day that teenager pelted my mother with a rock on Pelham Parkway, she didn't let me tiptoe back toward fear or sink down to those kids' level, and I'm a different man because of it. That day set my life on a new trajectory. I don't think my mother knew just how powerful or prophetic her words were. The look in her eyes and the tone of her voice solidified a spirit of resilience in me.

We don't try to cast out the darkness with more darkness; we turn the lights on.

We forgive even when the world tells us not to.

We don't just dip our toes in to feel how cold the water is; we jump in.

We ain't no half-steppers.

We jus' keep walkin', babee.

START A DIVERSITY GROUP

You made it all the way to the end of Part Four! By now, you've probably noticed this isn't a book about critiquing problems—it's a book about creating solutions.

Your final assignment is to be a part of the solution for your church by creating a Diversity Group. If your church already offers Diversity Groups, great! Let them know you are interested in jumping into the training and becoming a leader. However, every church approaches discipleship differently, so if your church doesn't offer Diversity Groups, *we are not telling you to march into your pastor's office and interrogate him or her.* You don't need to point out problems; just create a solution by building your own Diversity Group.

Pitch the idea to a diverse group of six to ten people. Invite them over for dinner and then ask them if they would be interested in continuing to meet once a week. If you enjoyed this book, why not read back through it with your group? Meet up to discuss one chapter each week by asking everyone these questions:

What did you like about the chapter? Why?

Was there anything you disagreed with in the chapter? What was it?

What is one practical step you are going to take this week in response to the chapter?

Or ask them to listen to an episode of our podcast, *Leadership in Black and White*, each week. Or dive into any of the other amazing books or resources that will push you all to learn more about each other and expand your understanding of diversity.

Try it for a semester and see how it goes. Who knows? Down the road, it may even become something your church wants to implement into its system!

Conclusion: Keep Open Hands

JOHN SIEBELING AND WAYNE FRANCIS

You have a race problem.

And we hope that by now, you see that we all do. The *House of God* is supposed to be a house that looks like heaven. And until we can say that is true for every congregation around the world, we all have work to do.

After all this talk about open hands, we feel the proper way to end this discussion, for now, is with one last hand illustration that many of us church folks grew up doing in our first Sunday School classes. You can find the hand motions on YouTube, but here are the words.

Here is the church.
Here is the steeple.
Open the doors and see all the people.

It's a cute little ditty, but when our kids say "see all the people," who are they picturing? Many churches have traded in steeples for more modern architecture, but have we also traded in homogeneity for diversity?

When we open the doors, do we see people of *all nations*? Are the seats filled with people who are Black, White, Asian, and Latino all worshiping together?

After all these chapters, we hope you realize that you not only have an opportunity to make a difference—you have a responsibility to try! Christians *can* and *should* be leading the way in these discussions about racial healing. The words we say, the things we post, the forgiveness we extend, the people we invite into our homes, and the churches we build should be reflecting a house that looks like heaven. When we do that, the world will listen!

There's an additional portion to this ditty:

Here's the parson going upstairs,
And here he is now, he's saying his prayers.

Would that we all pray the church will be a house that looks like heaven.

We used to teach this rhyme and hand game to children, and now our hope is the church will take the themes in this book and teach a new generation of people coming up how to relate to each other and love one another. It's not going to be easy. We may need to google "how to create a church with your fingers" to remember how to do it effectively, and it may take a little practice to get our fingers moving in the right direction. But with good *guidance*, coordination will come quickly. We are going to get there together:

One step at a time.

One word at a time.

One confession at a time.

One apology at a time.

One new experience at a time.

One collaboration at a time.

It's all work with our hands, isn't it? Every morning, we get to fold our hands and pray, and then every day we get to open our hands and get to work, laying aside our pride and our pain to come together. The journey may be long, but we are ready. Nobody can form a finger church with a fist. Our faith is high that open hands, open minds, and open hearts will let the doors of the church swing wide and show the world a house that looks like heaven.

Notes

Chapter 1: Start at the End

1. D'Vera Cohn, "It's Official: Minority Babies Are the Majority Among the Nation's Infants, but Only Just," Pew Research Center, June 23, 2016, https://www.pewresearch.org/fact-tank/2016/06/23/its-official-minority -babies-are-the-majority-among-the-nations-infants-but-only-just/.
2. Ezra Klein, *Why We're Polarized* (New York: Avid Reader Press, 2020), 72–73.

Chapter 2: Keep Walking

1. Aja Romano, "Why We Can't Stop Fighting About Cancel Culture," *Vox*, last updated August 25, 2020, https://www.vox.com/culture/2019/12/30/20879 720/what-is-cancel-culture-explained-history-debate.

Chapter 3: Get Ready

1. "Memphis Sanitation Workers' Strike," Stanford Martin Luther King, Jr., Research and Education Institute, https://kinginstitute.stanford.edu/encyclo pedia/memphis-sanitation-workers-strike.
2. "Two Sanitation Workers Killed," Memphis Public Libraries, February 3, 1968, https://www.memphislibrary.org/diversity/sanitation-strike-exhibit /sanitation-strike-exhibit-february-3-to-10-edition/two-sanitation- workers-killed/.
3. "'I've Been to the Mountaintop,' Address Delivered at Bishop Charles Mason Temple," Stanford Martin Luther King, Jr., Research and Education Institute, April 3, 1968, https://kinginstitute.stanford.edu/king-papers/documents /ive-been-mountaintop-address-delivered-bishop-charles-mason-temple.

Chapter 5: Check Your Posture

1. "White Privilege," Lexico, accessed August 30, 2020, https://www.lexico.com /en/definition/white_privilege.
2. "Woman's Viral 'Check Your Privilege' Challenge Is Opening People's Eyes," GMA, Good Morning America, June 9, 2020, https://www.good morningamerica.com/living/video/womans-viral-check-privilege-challenge -opening-peoples-eyes-71142398.

3. Amy Julia Becker, *White Picket Fences: Turning Toward Love in a World Divided by Privilege* (Colorado Springs: NavPress, 2018), 41–43.

4. Timothy B. Tyson, *The Blood of Emmett Till* (New York: Simon & Schuster, 2017), 1.

5. "The Trial of J. W. Milam and Roy Bryant," PBS, American Experience, accessed August 30, 2020, https://www.pbs.org/wgbh/americanexperience /features/emmett-trial-jw-milam-and-roy-bryant/.

6. Mamie Till-Mobley and Christopher Benson, *Death of Innocence: The Story of the Hate Crime That Changed America* (New York: Ballantine, 2005), 132.

7. Gina Kaufmann, "'It's A Very Heavy Kind of Grief'—Black Kansas Citians Reflect on Generations of Pain," KCUR 89.3, June 7, 2020, https://www .kcur.org/arts-life/2020-06-07/its-a-very-heavy-kind-of-grief-black-kansas -citians-reflect-on-generations-of-pain.

8. Jon Greenberg, "10 Examples That Prove White Privilege Exists in Every Aspect Imaginable," *Yes!* magazine, July 24, 2017, https://www.yesmagazine .org/social-justice/2017/07/24/10-examples-that-prove-white-privilege -exists-in-every-aspect-imaginable/.

9. "Letter from a Birmingham Jail [King, Jr.]," African Studies Center, University of Pennsylvania, April 16, 1963, https://www.africa.upenn.edu /Articles_Gen/Letter_Birmingham.html.

10. Reni Eddo-Lodge, *Why I'm No Longer Talking to White People About Race* (New York: Bloomsbury, 2019), 86.

11. The quotation is often attributed to Oklahoma coach Barry Switzer, but *The Yale Book of Quotations* (Fred R. Shapiro) tracks it to an earlier use in *Fortune* magazine in 1983 (New Haven: Yale Univ. Press, 2006), 358.

Chapter 6: Forgive, Don't Forget

1. Daniel McCoy, "The Killing of Botham Jean and 2 Kinds of Unthinkable," Renew.org, accessed June 8, 2021, https://renew.org/the-killing-of-botham -jean-and-2-kinds-of-unthinkable/.

2. Joshua Espinoza, "Amber Guyger Murder Trial Jurors Say the Recommended 28-Year Sentence Was Too 'Harsh,'" Complex, October 4, 2019, https://www.complex.com/life/2019/10/jurors-explain-amber-guyger -murder-trial-sentencing-decision.

3. Alicia C. Shepard, "A Mother's Courage," *The Washington Post*, January 11, 2003, https://www.washingtonpost.com/archive/opinions/2003/01/11 /a-mothers-courage/1fc4e451-cca2-4b12-b227-729d23295765/.

4. "What Oprah Knows for Sure About Doing Your Best," Oprah.com, accessed August 30, 2020, https://www.oprah.com/omagazine/what-oprah -knows-for-sure-about-doing-your-best.

Chapter 7: Check Your Vitals

1. C. S. Lewis, *Mere Christianity* (New York: HarperCollins, 2017), 134.

Chapter 8: Have an Open House

1. Megan Roby, "The Push and Pull Dynamics of White Flight: A Study of the Bronx Between 1950 and 1980," *Bronx County Historical Society Journal* XLV, nos. 1 and 2 (2008): 35–36, http://bronxhistoricalsociety.org/wp -content/uploads/2018/07/M.Roby_.pdf.

2. "Christians Are the Largest Religious Group in 2015," Pew Research Center, April 4, 2017, https://www.pewresearch.org/fact-tank/2017/04/05/christians-remain-worlds-largest-religious-group-but-they-are-declining-in-europe/ft_17-04-05_projectionsupdate_globalpop640px/.

3. "Resignation Letter," Bari Weiss, accessed August 30, 2020, https://www.bariweiss.com/resignation-letter.

Chapter 11: Pick Your Battles

1. Simon Kemp, "Digital 2020: Global Digital Overview," DataReportal, January 30, 2020, https://datareportal.com/reports/digital-2020-global-digital-overview.

2. Monica Anderson, Skye Toor, Lee Rainie, and Aaron Smith, "1. Public Attitudes Toward Political Engagement on Social Media," Pew Research Center, July 11, 2018, https://www.pewresearch.org/internet/2018/07/11/public-attitudes-toward-political-engagement-on-social-media/.

3. Kemp, "Digital 2020: Global Digital Overview."

4. Nicholas Thompson, "Tristan Harris: Tech Is 'Downgrading Humans.' It's Time to Fight Back," Wired, April 23, 2019, https://www.wired.com/story/tristan-harris-tech-is-downgrading-humans-time-to-fight-back/.

5. Melissa G. Hunt, Rachel Marx, Courtney Lipson, and Jordyn Young, "No More FOMO: Limiting Social Media Decreases Loneliness and Depression," *Journal of Social and Clinical Psychology* 37, no. 10 (December 2018): 751–768, https://doi.org/10.1521/jscp.2018.37.10.751.

6. Maeve Duggan, "Online Harassment," Pew Research Center, October 22, 2014, https://www.pewresearch.org/internet/2014/10/22/online-harassment/.

7. "Will Smith: 'Racism Is Not Getting Worse, It's Getting Filmed,'" *Hollywood Reporter*, August 3, 2016, https://www.hollywoodreporter.com/news/will-smith-colbert-race-relations-obama-politics-sings-summertime-916816.

Chapter 12: Take Inventory and Admit the Truth

1. Jemar Tisby, *The Color of Compromise: The Truth About the American Church's Complicity in Racism* (Grand Rapids: Zondervan, 2019), 53.

2. Quintard Taylor, *From Timbuktu to Katrina: Readings in African-American History, Volume 1* (Boston: Wadsworth Publishing, 2007), 45.

3. Dennis C. Dickerson, "Our History," African Methodist Episcopal Church, accessed June 10, 2021, https://www.ame-church.com/our-church/our-history/.

4. Martin L. King Jr., "Interview on 'Meet the Press,'" interview by Ned Brooks, Stanford Martin Luther King, Jr., Research and Education Institute, April 17, 1960, https://kinginstitute.stanford.edu/king-papers/documents/interview-meet-press.

5. Jonathan M. Yeager, *Early Evangelicalism: A Reader* (Oxford: Oxford Univ. Press, 2013), 379.

6. Paulette Brown-Hinds, "Race, Religion and the Azusa Street Revival," bvn, Black Voice News, May 8, 2006, https://www.blackvoicenews.com/2006/05/08/race-religion-and-the-azusa-street-revival/.

7. Joe Creech, "Visions of Glory: The Place of the Azusa Street Revival in Pentecostal History," *Church History* 65, no. 3 (1996): 412, July 28, 2009, https://doi.org/10.2307/3169938.

Chapter 13: Follow a King, Not a Politician

1. D. A. Carson, *Love in Hard Places* (Wheaton, IL: Crossway, 2002), 61.
2. "A Knock at Midnight," Stanford Martin Luther King, Jr., Research and Education Institute, June 5, 1963, https://kinginstitute.stanford.edu/king -papers/documents/knock-midnight.
3. Jemar Tisby, *The Color of Compromise: The Truth About the American Church's Complicity in Racism* (Grand Rapids: Zondervan, 2019), 54.
4. Scott Sauls, "Stepping Away from Un-Christian Politics," *Scott Sauls* (blog), August 14, 2020, https://scottsauls.com/blog/2020/08/14/unchristian -politics/.
5. John Wesley, *The Journal of the Rev. John Wesley, A.M., Sometime Fellow of Lincoln College, Oxford*, vol. 4 (London: Wesleyan Conference Office, 1867), 29.

New Video Study for Your Church or Small Group

If you've enjoyed this book, now you can go deeper with the companion video Bible study!

In this five-session study, John Siebling and Wayne Francis help you apply the principles in *God and Race* to your life. The study guide includes streaming video access, video teaching notes, group discussion questions, personal reflection questions, and a leader's guide.

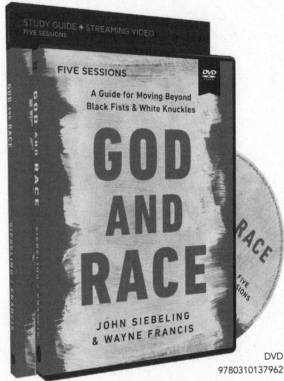

Study Guide plus
Streaming Video
9780310137948

DVD
9780310137962

Available now at your favorite bookstore,
or streaming video on StudyGateway.com.

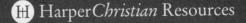
HarperChristian Resources